M000106248

On Course: Mapping Instruction
A Teacher's Guide for Planning

for
Holt Literature & Language Arts
Holt Handbook

- **Flowcharts for Planning Instruction**
- **Lesson Plans with Standards Correlations**

HOLT, RINEHART AND WINSTON

A Harcourt Classroom Education Company

Austin · New York · Orlando · Atlanta · San Francisco · Boston · Dallas · Toronto · London

STAFF CREDITS

EDITORIAL

Manager of Operations
Bill Wahlgren

Executive Editor
Emily Shenk

Senior Editor
Cheryl L. Christian

Writing and Editing

Janis D. Russell, *Editor*

Copyediting

Michael Neibergall, *Copyediting Manager;* Mary Malone, *Copyediting Supervisor;* Joel Bourgeois, Elizabeth Dickson, Emily Force, Julie A. Hill, Julia Thomas Hu, Jennifer Kirkland, Millicent Ondras, Dennis Scharnberg, *Copyeditors*

Project Administration

Marie Price, *Managing Editor;* Lori De La Garza, *Editorial Operations Coordinator;* Heather Cheyne, Mark Holland, Marcus Johnson, Jennifer Renteria, Janet Riley, Kelly Tankersley, *Project Administration;* Ruth Hooker, Joie Pickett, Margaret Sanchez, *Word Processing*

ART, DESIGN AND PHOTO

Graphic Services

Kristen Darby, *Manager*
Jeff Robinson, *Senior Ancillary Designer*
Eric Rupprath, *Designer*

Image Acquisitions

Joe London, *Director;* Jeannie Taylor, *Photo Research Supervisor;* Tim Taylor, *Photo Research Supervisor;* Rick Benavides, *Photo Researcher;* Cindy Verheyden, *Senior Photo Researcher;* Elaine Tate, *Supervisor*

Cover Design

Curtis Riker, *Director*
Sunday Patterson, *Designer*

PRODUCTION

Belinda Barbosa Lopez, *Senior Production Coordinator*
Carol Trammal, *Production Supervisor*
Beth Prevelige, *Prepress Manager*

MANUFACTURING/INVENTORY

Shirley Cantrell, *Supervisor of Inventory and Manufacturing*
Wilonda Ieans, *Manufacturing Coordinator*
Mark McDonald, *Inventory Planner*

ISBN 0–03–066118-8

3   179   03

Table of Contents

Table of Contents (continued)

To the Teacher

Holt Literature & Language Arts provides you with comprehensive coverage of the California Standards. The Pupil's Edition addresses the Standards for reading literature selections and informational materials (Part 1) and for writing, listening, and speaking (Part 2). The *Holt Handbook* covers the Standards for English-language conventions.

On Course provides you with a road map to using *Holt Literature & Language Arts* to teach the concepts and skills required by the California Standards. The content is divided into quarters to allow students sufficient time to master each Standard and to prepare for quarterly standards-based assessments.

How does *On Course* help me plan my lessons?

On Course shows you what material to cover in each quarter in order to ensure that all Standards are covered in the course of a year. Overviews of the year, of each quarter, and of each chapter help you chart your path through the program. *On Course* also provides weekly lesson plans, along with pacing suggestions, that you can tailor to meet your students' needs.

What planning tools does *On Course* provide?

- **Year at a Glance** This map gives you a quick look at the year by showing you which chapters and workshops should be taught in each quarter to provide comprehensive coverage of the Standards. It also indicates when to administer the standards-based assessments required by California and provided in *Diagnostic & Summative Assessments.*

- **Quarter Overviews** These pages show how the chapters in the *Holt Handbook* may be taught in conjunction with the *Holt Literature & Language Arts* Pupil's Edition.

- **Chapter Overviews** These pages provide more specific information on the Pupil's Edition chapters and workshops, along with specific lessons from the *Holt Handbook.* Page references are provided for easy navigation through the program.

How do the Lesson Plans simplify my lesson planning?

- **Pacing guide** The weekly Lesson Plans help you pace instruction by suggesting material to be taught and assessed each week.

- **Resources lists** The Plans list Pupil's Edition lessons, *Holt Handbook* lessons, and the ancillaries that accompany them.

- **Standards information** The Standards covered in a given week are listed at the top of the lesson plan.

- **Teaching suggestions** Notes at the bottom of the weekly plans provide you with alternatives and suggest ways to reinforce mastery of the Standards.

- **Check boxes** These help you customize the Plans and record exactly which feature of the program you have covered or plan to cover.

- **Tinted backgrounds** A quick look at the background tint shows you which book is referenced. The turquoise background designates the *Holt Literature & Language Arts* Pupil's Edition and the ancillary features that support it. The green background designates the *Holt Handbook* and supporting ancillary material.

What if I don't have time to teach everything listed in a week?

- **Minimum Course of Study** The features in red type represent the minimum course of study required to meet the California Standards. You may direct students having difficulty to concentrate only on these selections and lessons so they can successfully master the Standards. Students on grade level may complete most or all of the assignments listed in a week. Advanced students may read all of the selections and continue with independent reading. The Lesson Plans allow you flexibility to tailor the week's lessons according to student needs.

- **Diagnostic Previews** Use the Diagnostic Previews in the *Holt Handbook* to determine what students already know about English-language conventions and to help you assess which lessons should be taught in a chapter.

How do I address the learning needs of different students?

The ancillaries listed under Standards-Based Components give all students access to standards-based instruction.

- *Interactive Reading* anticipates and remediates problems that some students may encounter when reading the selections in Part 1 of *Holt Literature & Language Arts* Pupil's Edition.

- *Lesson Plans for Language Development* offers teaching strategies for English-language learners and special education students. It covers the reading selections; the Writing, the Listening and Speaking, and the Media Workshops; and *Holt Handbook* chapters.

- *Writing, Listening, & Speaking* guides students who need help with the concepts covered in the workshops and mini-workshops, as well as offering on-level students additional support and advanced students enrichment activities.

- *Developmental Language & Sentence Skills* offers further instruction to help students having difficulty mastering English-language conventions. The first items in the practice exercises provide students with prompts to help them analyze the task.

- *Language & Sentence Skills Practice*, in addition to providing practice for On-Level Learners, has extension activities that Advanced Learners may use.

The Lesson Plans also designate the learning level for particular worksheets:

- **LHD** for Learners Having Difficulty and for on-level students who experience trouble mastering a particular concept
- **OLL** for On-Level Learners
- **AL** for Advanced Learners

How do I assess student progress?

Holt Literature & Language Arts provides several ways for you to assess progress. Assessment options listed in the Lesson Plans include both ongoing and summative assessments.

- **Entry-Level Diagnostic Test** Administered at the beginning of the year, this test identifies which prerequisite skills students have learned. Summative tests at the end of every quarter confirm whether a student has mastered the Standards taught in that quarter. These tests are provided in *Diagnostic & Summative Assessments.*

- **Reading Selection Tests, Chapter Tests, and Workshop Tests** These tests help students prepare for the summative assessments and allow teachers to determine what extra help students need. These tests are located in the *Progress Assessment* booklets.

- **Analytic Scales and Scoring Rubrics** These instruments are evaluation tools for writing, listening, and speaking. They appear in *Progress Assessment: Writing, Listening, & Speaking.* For ongoing assessment, distribute the scales and rubrics to students as they begin a workshop. This enables students to engage in both peer and self-evaluation, as well as to see exactly how you will be evaluating their work. It also allows you to check their work as they progress through a workshop.

Minimum Course of Study

Year at a Glance

FIRST QUARTER

 DIAGNOSTIC & SUMMATIVE ASSESSMENTS — Entry-Level Test

 HOLT LITERATURE & LANGUAGE ARTS — **Chapter 1** / **Workshop 1** / Mini-Workshop 3

 HOLT HANDBOOK — **Chapters 1–3**

 DIAGNOSTIC & SUMMATIVE ASSESSMENTS — First-Quarter Test

SECOND QUARTER

 HOLT LITERATURE & LANGUAGE ARTS — **Chapters 2–3** / **Workshop 2** / Mini-Workshops 1 and 5

 HOLT HANDBOOK — **Chapters 4–8**

 DIAGNOSTIC & SUMMATIVE ASSESSMENTS — Midyear Test

THIRD QUARTER

 HOLT LITERATURE & LANGUAGE ARTS — **Chapters 4–5** / **Workshop 3** / Mini-Workshop 4

 HOLT HANDBOOK — **Chapters 9–12**

 DIAGNOSTIC & SUMMATIVE ASSESSMENTS — Third-Quarter Test

FOURTH QUARTER

 HOLT LITERATURE & LANGUAGE ARTS — **Chapters 6–7** / **Workshops 4–5** / Mini-Workshop 2

 HOLT HANDBOOK — **Chapters 13–16 and 18**

 DIAGNOSTIC & SUMMATIVE ASSESSMENTS — End-of-Year Test

First-Quarter Overview

DIAGNOSTIC & SUMMATIVE ASSESSMENTS

3 days

Entry-Level Test pp. 6–40

HOLT LITERATURE & LANGUAGE ARTS

15 days

Chapter 1
Structures: Clarifying Meaning pp. 2–103

12 days

Workshop 1
Narration

Writing a Short Story pp. 536–557

Giving and Listening to an Oral Narrative pp. 558–562

4 days

Mini-Workshop 3
Writing a Descriptive Essay pp. 700–703

HOLT HANDBOOK

Chapter 1
The Parts of a Sentence pp. 2–23

Chapter 2
Parts of Speech Overview:
Noun, Pronoun, Adjective pp. 24–43

Chapter 3
Parts of Speech Overview:
Verb, Adverb, Preposition, Conjunction, Interjection pp. 44–71

DIAGNOSTIC & SUMMATIVE ASSESSMENTS

1 day

First-Quarter Test pp. 41–59

Second-Quarter Overview

HOLT LITERATURE & LANGUAGE ARTS

12 days

Chapter 2
Characters: Living Many Lives pp. 104–155

13 days

Workshop 2
Response to Literature

Writing a Character Analysis pp. 566–582

Giving and Listening to an Oral Summary pp. 583–587

Analyzing Electronic Journalism pp. 588–594

11 days

Chapter 3
Themes Across Time
pp. 156–219

4 days

Mini-Workshop 1
Analyzing Cause and Effect pp. 694–696

4 days

Mini-Workshop 5
Analyzing a Documentary p. 707

HOLT HANDBOOK

Chapter 4
Complements pp. 72–87

Chapter 5
The Phrase pp. 88–111

Chapter 6
The Clause pp. 112–127

Chapter 7
Kinds of Sentence Structure pp. 128–145

Chapter 8
Agreement pp. 146–173

DIAGNOSTIC & SUMMATIVE ASSESSMENTS

Midyear Test pp. 60–78

1 day

Third-Quarter Overview

 HOLT LITERATURE & LANGUAGE ARTS

 HOLT HANDBOOK

16 days

Chapter 4
Point of View: Who's Talking?
pp. 220–303

Chapter 9
Using Verbs Correctly
pp. 174–199

4 days

Mini-Workshop 4
Writing an Autobiographical Narrative pp. 704–706

Chapter 10
Using Pronouns Correctly
pp. 200–221

16 days

Chapter 5
Worlds of Words: Prose and Poetry
pp. 304–409

Chapter 11
Using Modifiers Correctly
pp. 222–243

8 days

Workshop 3
Persuasion
Writing a Persuasive Essay
pp. 598–615

Giving and Listening to a Persuasive Speech pp. 616–622

Chapter 12
A Glossary of Usage
pp. 244–263

 DIAGNOSTIC & SUMMATIVE ASSESSMENTS

Third-Quarter Test pp. 79–97

1 day

4

Fourth-Quarter Overview

 HOLT LITERATURE & LANGUAGE ARTS

HOLT HANDBOOK

16 days

Chapter 6
Where I Stand: Literary Criticism pp. 410–479

Chapter 13
Capital Letters pp. 264–287

14 days

Workshop 4
Research

Writing a Research Report pp. 626–653

Giving and Listening to an Informative Speech pp. 654–660

Chapter 14
Punctuation: End Marks, Commas, Semicolons, and Colons pp. 288–317

5 days

Mini-Workshop 2
Documenting Reference Sources pp. 697–699

Chapter 15
Punctuation: Underlining (Italics), Quotation Marks, Apostrophes, Hyphens, Parentheses, Brackets, and Dashes pp. 318–345

13 days

Chapter 7
Reading for Life pp. 480–507

Chapter 16
Spelling pp. 346–375

5 days

Workshop 5
Writing to Learn

Learning Through Writing pp. 663-680

Chapter 18
Writing Effective Sentences pp. 412–443

Lesson Plans for teaching Chapter 17: Correcting Common Errors are noted throughout the year. See Review notes.

 DIAGNOSTIC & SUMMATIVE ASSESSMENTS

End-of-Year Test pp. 98–125

2 days

Chapter 1 Overview
with Workshop 1, Mini-Workshop 3, *Holt Handbook*

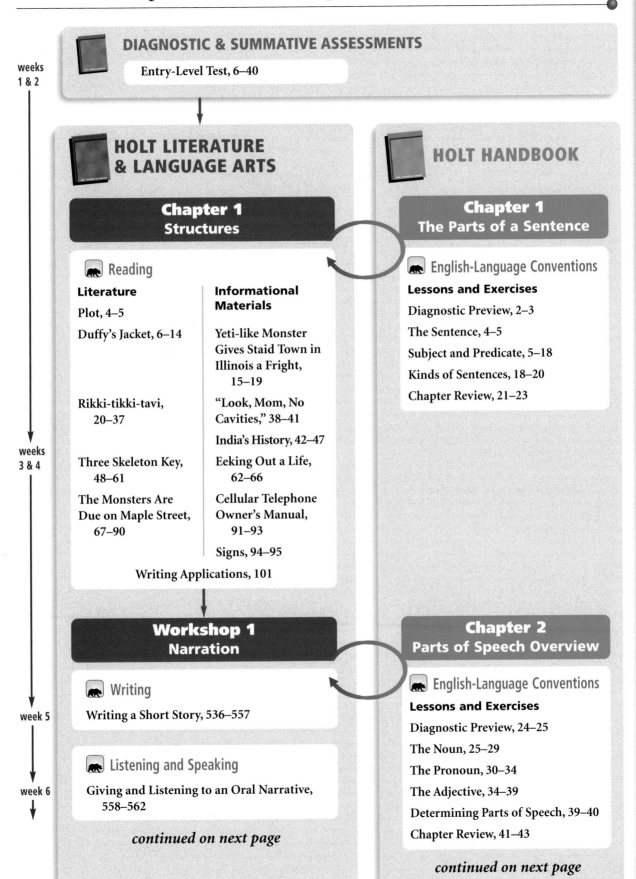

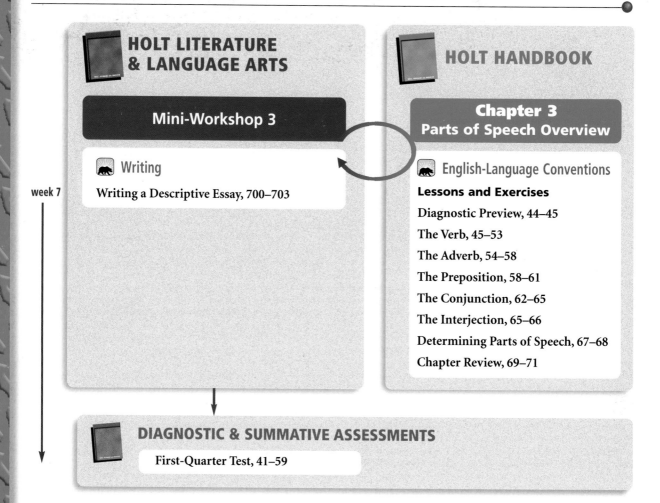

HOLT LITERATURE & LANGUAGE ARTS

Mini-Workshop 3

Writing

Writing a Descriptive Essay, 700–703

week 7

HOLT HANDBOOK

Chapter 3
Parts of Speech Overview

English-Language Conventions

Lessons and Exercises

Diagnostic Preview, 44–45

The Verb, 45–53

The Adverb, 54–58

The Preposition, 58–61

The Conjunction, 62–65

The Interjection, 65–66

Determining Parts of Speech, 67–68

Chapter Review, 69–71

DIAGNOSTIC & SUMMATIVE ASSESSMENTS

First-Quarter Test, 41–59

GRADE 7: PUPIL'S EDITION AND HOLT HANDBOOK	STANDARDS-BASED COMPONENTS	SUPPORTING RESOURCES
ASSESSMENT		**One-Stop Planner**
Diagnostic & Summative Assessments ❑ Entry-Level Test pp. 6–40		❑ Test Generator
Chapter 1: Structures ❑ Plot pp. 4–5 **Reading Matters** ❑ Strategy Lesson 1: Summarizing the Plot pp. 510–511	**Interactive Reading** ❑ Strategy Launch and Practice Read pp. 1–11 **Lesson Plans for Language Development** ❑ pp. 3–4	❑ **One-Stop Planner** **At Home: A Guide to Standards Mastery** ❑ Discussing Stories with Your Child: Plot p. 5 ❑ **One-Stop Planner**

Literature
❑ Duffy's Jacket pp. 6–14
  ❑ Before You Read p. 6
  ❑ Focus On: questions and activities p. 13
  ❑ Vocabulary: Clarifying Word Meanings p. 14
	Interactive Reading
	❑ p. 12
	
	Lesson Plans for Language Development
	❑ pp. 5–8, 26
	
	Vocabulary Development
	❑ p. 1
		❑ **Audio CD Library**
		❑ **One-Stop Planner**

Progress Assessment: Reading, Vocabulary, & Literature ❑ Duffy's Jacket pp. 1–3		**One-Stop Planner** ❑ Test Generator
Chapter 1: The Parts of a Sentence ❑ Diagnostic Preview pp. 2–3	**Language & Sentence Skills Practice** ❑ Choices p. 1	❑ **One-Stop Planner**
	Spelling Lessons & Activities ❑ Lesson 1: Spelling Compound Words pp. x–1	❑ **One-Stop Planner**

*(Left vertical labels: **HOLT LITERATURE & LANGUAGE ARTS**, **HOLT HANDBOOK**)*

OPTIONAL *Daily Language Activities Transparencies*
Transparency 87   Critical Reading: Sentence Completions

• **Red type** = Minimum Course of Study necessary to meet the California Standards
• **LHD** = Learners Having Difficulty (Benchmark/Strategic) **OLL** = On-Level Learners **AL** = Advanced Learners

GRADE 7: PUPIL'S EDITION AND HOLT HANDBOOK	STANDARDS–BASED COMPONENTS	SUPPORTING RESOURCES
Chapter 1: Structures, cont. **Informational Material** ❏ Yeti-like Monster Gives Staid Town in Illinois a Fright pp. 15–19 ❏ Reading Informational Materials p. 15 ❏ Focus On: questions p. 18 ❏ Vocabulary: Clarifying Word Meanings p. 19	**Interactive Reading** ❏ p. 13 **Lesson Plans for Language Development** ❏ pp. 9, 27, 35 **Vocabulary Development** ❏ p. 2	❏ **Audio CD Library** ❏ **One-Stop Planner**
Progress Assessment: Reading, Vocabulary, & Literature ❏ Yeti-like Monster Gives Staid Town in Illinois a Fright pp. 4–5		**One-Stop Planner** ❏ Test Generator
Chapter 1: Structures, cont. **Literature** ❏ Rikki-tikki-tavi pp. 20–37 ❏ Before You Read p. 20 ❏ Focus On: questions and activities p. 36 ❏ Vocabulary: Clarifying Word Meanings p. 37 **Reading Matters** ❏ Strategy Lesson 7: Using Context Clues pp. 524–525	**Interactive Reading** ❏ p. 14 **Lesson Plans for Language Development** ❏ pp. 10–13, 28 **Vocabulary Development** ❏ p. 3	❏ **Audio CD Library** **Visual Connections** ❏ Videocassette Segment 1 ❏ **One-Stop Planner**
Progress Assessment: Reading, Vocabulary, & Literature ❏ Rikki-tikki-tavi pp. 6–8		**One-Stop Planner** ❏ Test Generator
Chapter 1: Structures, cont. **Informational Material** ❏ "Look, Mom, No Cavities" pp. 38–41 ❏ Reading Informational Materials p. 38 ❏ Focus On: questions p. 40 ❏ Vocabulary: Words from Latin p. 41 **Reading Matters** ❏ Strategy Lesson 7: Using Context Clues pp. 524–525	**Interactive Reading** ❏ p. 15 **Lesson Plans for Language Development** ❏ pp. 14, 29 **Vocabulary Development** ❏ p. 4	❏ **Audio CD Library** ❏ **One-Stop Planner**
Progress Assessment: Reading, Vocabulary, & Literature ❏ "Look, Mom, No Cavities" pp. 9–10		**One-Stop Planner** ❏ Test Generator

HOLT LITERATURE & LANGUAGE ARTS

• **Red type** = Minimum Course of Study necessary to meet the California Standards
• **LHD** = Learners Having Difficulty (Benchmark/Strategic) **OLL** = On-Level Learners **AL** = Advanced Learners

	GRADE 7: PUPIL'S EDITION AND HOLT HANDBOOK	STANDARDS-BASED COMPONENTS	SUPPORTING RESOURCES
HOLT LIT & LANGUAGE ARTS	**Chapter 1: Structures,** cont. **Informational Material** ❑ India's History pp. 42–47 　❑ Reading Informational Materials p. 42 　❑ Focus On: questions p. 47	**Interactive Reading** ❑ p. 16 **Lesson Plans for Language Development** ❑ pp. 15, 30, 36	❑ **Audio CD Library** ❑ **One-Stop Planner**
	Progress Assessment: Reading, Vocabulary, & Literature ❑ India's History pp. 11–12		**One-Stop Planner** ❑ Test Generator
HOLT HANDBOOK	**Chapter 1: The Parts of a Sentence,** cont. ❑ The Sentence pp. 4–5 ❑ Subject and Predicate: The Subject pp. 5–8 ❑ Subject and Predicate: The Predicate pp. 8–11 ❑ Subject and Predicate: The Verb Phrase pp. 11–12	**Developmental Language & Sentence Skills** ❑ LHD pp. 1–2, Exercises A & B pp. 3–6 **Language & Sentence Skills Practice** ❑ OLL pp. 2–9 **Lesson Plans for Language Development** ❑ pp. 272–273	❑ **One-Stop Planner**
		Spelling Lessons & Activities ❑ Lesson 2: Spelling Homophones pp. 2–3	❑ **One-Stop Planner**
			At Home: A Guide to Standards Mastery ❑ Getting Your Child to Complete Homework p. 3 ❑ Helping Your Child Prepare for Tests p. 4 ❑ **One-Stop Planner**

OPTIONAL　*Daily Language Activities Transparencies*

Transparency 95　Critical Reading: Passage Completions
Transparency 35　Vocabulary: Syno-grams

Standards Reinforcement: For students needing more help mastering Reading Standard 3.2, teach "Rikki-tikki-tavi."

GRADE 7: PUPIL'S EDITION AND HOLT HANDBOOK	STANDARDS-BASED COMPONENTS	SUPPORTING RESOURCES

Chapter 1: Structures, cont.
 	
Literature
❑ Three Skeleton Key pp. 48–61
  ❑ Before You Read p. 48
  ❑ Focus On: questions and activities p. 60
  ❑ Vocabulary: Clarifying Word Meanings p. 61
	Interactive Reading
	❑ p. 17
	Lesson Plans for Language Development
	❑ pp. 16–19, 31
	Vocabulary Development
	❑ p. 5
		❑ **Audio CD Library**
		Fine Art Transparencies
		❑ Transparency 1
		At Home: A Guide to Standards Mastery
		❑ Practicing Fluency with Your Child: Reading Plays Aloud p. 8
		❑ **One-Stop Planner**

Progress Assessment: Reading, Vocabulary, & Literature ❑ Three Skeleton Key pp. 13–15		**One-Stop Planner** ❑ Test Generator

Chapter 1: Structures, cont.
 	
Informational Material
❑ Eeking Out a Life pp. 62–66
  ❑ Reading Informational Materials p. 62
  ❑ Focus On: questions p. 65
  ❑ Grammar Link: Subject-Verb Agreement Is Unanimous! p. 66
	Interactive Reading
	❑ p. 18
	Lesson Plans for Language Development
	❑ pp. 20, 32, 37
	Vocabulary Development
	❑ p. 6
		❑ **Audio CD Library**
		❑ **One-Stop Planner**

Progress Assessment: Reading, Vocabulary, & Literature ❑ Eeking Out a Life pp. 16–17		**One-Stop Planner** ❑ Test Generator

Chapter 1: Structures, cont.
 	
Literature
❑ The Monsters Are Due on Maple Street pp. 67–90
  ❑ Before You Read pp. 67–68
  ❑ Act One pp. 69–79
    ❑ Focus On: questions p. 78
    ❑ Vocabulary: Clarifying Word Meanings p. 79
  ❑ Act Two pp. 80–90
    ❑ Focus On: questions and activities pp. 88–89
    ❑ Vocabulary: Clarifying Word Meanings p. 90
	Interactive Reading
	❑ p. 19
	Lesson Plans for Language Development
	❑ pp. 21–24, 33
	Vocabulary Development
	❑ p. 7
		❑ **Audio CD Library**
		❑ **One-Stop Planner**

Progress Assessment: Reading, Vocabulary, & Literature ❑ The Monsters Are Due on Maple Street pp. 18–21		**One-Stop Planner** ❑ Test Generator

HOLT LITERATURE & LANGUAGE ARTS

• **Red type** = Minimum Course of Study necessary to meet the California Standards
• **LHD** = Learners Having Difficulty (Benchmark/Strategic) **OLL** = On-Level Learners **AL** = Advanced Learners

GRADE 7: PUPIL'S EDITION AND HOLT HANDBOOK	STANDARDS-BASED COMPONENTS	SUPPORTING RESOURCES
Chapter 1: The Parts of a Sentence, cont. ❏ Subject and Predicate: Finding the Subject p. 13 ❏ Subject and Predicate: Compound Subjects and Compound Verbs pp. 13–18 ❏ Kinds of Sentences pp. 18–20 ❏ Chapter Review pp. 21–23	**Developmental Language & Sentence Skills** ❏ LHD Exercise C pp. 4 and 6, 7–8 **Language & Sentence Skills Practice** ❏ OLL pp. 10–20 **Lesson Plans for Language Development** ❏ pp. 272–273	❏ **One-Stop Planner**
ASSESSMENT **Progress Assessment:** *Holt Handbook* ❏ Chapter 1 Test pp. 1–2		**One-Stop Planner** ❏ Test Generator
	Spelling Lessons & Activities ❏ Lesson 3: Adding Endings to Words pp. 4–5	❏ **One-Stop Planner**

HOLT HANDBOOK

OPTIONAL *Daily Language Activities Transparencies*

Transparency 23   Vocabulary: Connotations
Transparency 103   Critical Reading: Passage Analysis

Minimum Course of Study: To allow more time for "Cellular Telephone Owner's Manual" teach it this week instead of during Week 4.

Teaching Notes

GRADE 7: PUPIL'S EDITION AND HOLT HANDBOOK	STANDARDS-BASED COMPONENTS	SUPPORTING RESOURCES

Chapter 1: Structures, cont.
 	
Informational Material
❑ Cellular Telephone Owner's Manual pp. 91–93
  ❑ Reading Informational Materials p. 91
  ❑ Focus On: questions and activity p. 93
	Interactive Reading
	❑ p. 20
	Lesson Plans for Language Development
	❑ pp. 25, 34, 38
		At Home: A Guide to Standards Mastery
		❑ Reinforcing Reading Comprehension: Following Technical Directions p. 11
		
		❑ **One-Stop Planner**

Progress Assessment: Reading, Vocabulary, & Literature ❑ Cellular Telephone Owner's Manual pp. 22–23		**One-Stop Planner** ❑ Test Generator
Chapter 1: Structures, cont. **Informational Material** ❑ Signs pp. 94–95 ❑ Reading Informational Materials p. 94	**Interactive Reading** ❑ p. 21	❑ **One-Stop Planner**
	Interactive Reading ❑ AL The Elephant's Child pp. 22–33, 34 ❑ OLL *from* Guide to Mammals pp. 35–39, 40 ❑ LHD The Monkey and the Crocodile pp. 41–44, 45	❑ **One-Stop Planner**
Chapter 1: Structures, cont. **Standards Review** ❑ Literary Response and Analysis pp. 96–97 ❑ Reading Comprehension pp. 98–99 ❑ Test Practice: Vocabulary Development p. 100	**Vocabulary Development** ❑ p. 8	❑ **One-Stop Planner**

ASSESSMENT
Progress Assessment: Reading, Vocabulary, & Literature
❑ Chapter Test
  ❑ Part A: Literary Response and Analysis pp. 24–25
  ❑ Part B: Reading Application pp. 26–31
		One-Stop Planner
		❑ Test Generator

Chapter 1: Structures, cont. ❑ Writing Applications: Short Story p. 101		

HOLT LITERATURE & LANGUAGE ARTS

• **Red type** = Minimum Course of Study necessary to meet the California Standards
• **LHD** = Learners Having Difficulty (Benchmark/Strategic)   **OLL** = On-Level Learners   **AL** = Advanced Learners

GRADE 7: PUPIL'S EDITION AND HOLT HANDBOOK	STANDARDS-BASED COMPONENTS	SUPPORTING RESOURCES
Workshop 1: Narration **Writing a Short Story** ❑ Professional Model: A Short Story pp. 536–542 Prewriting pp. 542–548 ❑ Practice & Apply 1–2 pp. 543, 548	**Writing, Listening, & Speaking** ❑ LHD Journal Warm-up: Short Story Transparency 5 ❑ LHD Prewriting: Short-Story Writing Prompt Transparency 6 ❑ OLL Prewriting pp. 2, 5 ❑ Prewriting: Short-Story Writing Prompts p. 3 ❑ OLL Using Narrative Strategies p. 4 **Lesson Plans for Language Development** ❑ p. 249	❑ **One-Stop Planner**
Chapter 1: The Parts of a Sentence, cont. ❑ Writing Application p. 23	**Language & Sentence Skills Practice** ❑ AL Literary Model pp. 21–22 ❑ AL Writing Application p. 23	❑ **One-Stop Planner**
	Spelling Lessons & Activities ❑ Lesson 4: Words from Spanish pp. 6–7	❑ **One-Stop Planner**

Side tabs: HOLT LITERATURE & LANGUAGE ARTS / HOLT HANDBOOK

OPTIONAL *Daily Language Activities Transparencies*

Transparency 31   Vocabulary: Frequently Confused Words
Transparency 50   Analogies: Mixed

Teaching Notes

GRADE 7: PUPIL'S EDITION AND HOLT HANDBOOK	STANDARDS-BASED COMPONENTS	SUPPORTING RESOURCES

HOLT LITERATURE & LANGUAGE ARTS
 	
Workshop 1: Narration, cont.
 	
Writing a Short Story
Prewriting pp. 548–549
   ❑ Practice & Apply 3 p. 549
 	
Writing pp. 550–552
   ❑ Practice & Apply 4 p. 550
 	
Revising pp. 553–555
   ❑ Practice & Apply 5 p. 555
	Writing, Listening, & Speaking
	❑ OLL Prewriting pp. 6–7
	❑ LHD Think Sheet p. 8
	❑ LHD, OLL Writing p. 9
	❑ Revising Transparency 1
	❑ Revised Draft Transparency 2
	❑ OLL Revising p. 10
	❑ AL Revising Practice p. 11
	❑ Revising: Evaluate Short Stories p. 12
	❑ OLL Precise Nouns and Adjectives p. 13
	
	Lesson Plans for Language Development
	❑ pp. 249–250
	
	Progress Assessment: Writing, Listening, & Speaking [for help with revising and self-evaluation]
	❑ Analytical Scale and Scoring Rubric pp. 30–32
	❑ General Scales and Sample Papers pp. 70–85
		At Home: A Guide to Standards Mastery
		❑ Helping Your Child Write a Short Story pp. 17–18
		
		❑ **One-Stop Planner**

HOLT HANDBOOK **Chapter 2: Parts of Speech Overview** ❑ Diagnostic Preview pp. 24–25 ❑ The Noun pp. 25–29 ❑ The Pronoun pp. 30–34	**Developmental Language & Sentence Skills** ❑ LHD pp. 9–16 **Language & Sentence Skills Practice** ❑ Choices p. 24 ❑ OLL pp. 25–33 **Lesson Plans for Language Development** ❑ p. 274	❑ **One-Stop Planner**
	Spelling Lessons & Activities ❑ Lesson 5: Music Words pp. 8–9	❑ **One-Stop Planner**

OPTIONAL *Daily Language Activities Transparencies*

Transparency 1	Proofreading Warm-ups
Transparency 49	Analogies: Noun : Quality
Transparency 79	Sentence Combining

Week 6
Lesson Plan

Writing 1.6, 2.0, 2.1c
Listening & Speaking 1.0, 1.2, 1.4, 1.5, 1.6, 1.7, 2.0, 2.1, 2.1a, 2.1b, 2.1c
English-Language Conventions 1.0, 1.3, 1.4

GRADE 7: PUPIL'S EDITION AND HOLT HANDBOOK	STANDARDS-BASED COMPONENTS	SUPPORTING RESOURCES
Writing Workshop 1: Narration, cont. **Writing a Short Story** Publishing pp. 556–557 ❏ Grammar Link: Punctuating Dialogue p. 556 ❏ Practice & Apply 6 p. 557	**Writing, Listening, & Speaking** ❏ OLL Proofreading p. 14 ❏ Proofreading Transparency 3 ❏ Proofread Draft Transparency 4 **Lesson Plans for Language Development** ❏ p. 250	❏ **One-Stop Planner**
ASSESSMENT **Progress Assessment: Writing, Listening, & Speaking** ❏ Writing Workshop 1 Test pp. 2–4 ❏ Analytical Scale and Scoring Rubric pp. 30–32 ❏ General Scales and Sample Papers pp. 70–85		❏ **One-Stop Planner**
Workshop 1: Narration, cont. **Giving and Listening to an Oral Narrative** ❏ Select a Story pp. 558–559 ❏ Plan Your Presentation pp. 559–561 ❏ Rehearse p. 561 ❏ Respond to an Oral Narrative p. 562 ❏ Practice & Apply 7 p. 562	**Writing, Listening, & Speaking** ❏ Project-Planning Guide p. 18 ❏ OLL Think Sheet p. 19 ❏ AL Delivery I and II pp. 20–21 ❏ LHD Sample Notecards Transparency 7 ❏ Evaluation Guide p. 22 ❏ Video Think Sheet p. 23 **Lesson Plans for Language Development** ❏ p. 251	**Writing, Listening, & Speaking** ❏ Videocassette Segment 1 **At Home: A Guide to Standards Mastery** ❏ Listening and Speaking: What Parents Can Do to Help pp. 15–16 ❏ **One-Stop Planner**
Progress Assessment: Writing, Listening, & Speaking ❏ Analytical Scale and Scoring Rubric pp. 33–35		❏ **One-Stop Planner**
Workshop 1: Narration, cont. ❏ Standards Practice and Review p. 563		

	Writing, Listening, & Speaking
	❏ Choices p. 24
	  ❏ LHD Art
	  ❏ OLL Writing, Social Studies
	  ❏ AL Careers
		❏ **One-Stop Planner**

HOLT LITERATURE & LANGUAGE ARTS

- **Red type** = Minimum Course of Study necessary to meet the California Standards
- **LHD** = Learners Having Difficulty (Benchmark/Strategic)   **OLL** = On-Level Learners   **AL** = Advanced Learners

Week 6, continued
Lesson Plan

Writing 1.6, 2.0, 2.1c
Listening & Speaking 1.0, 1.2, 1.4, 1.5, 1.6, 1.7, 2.0, 2.1,
2.1a, 2.1b, 2.1c
English-Language Conventions 1.0, 1.3, 1.4

GRADE 7: PUPIL'S EDITION AND HOLT HANDBOOK	STANDARDS–BASED COMPONENTS	SUPPORTING RESOURCES
Chapter 2: Parts of Speech Overview, cont. ❑ The Adjective pp. 34–39 ❑ Determining Parts of Speech pp. 39–40 ❑ Chapter Review pp. 41–43 ❑ Writing Application p. 43	**Developmental Language & Sentence Skills** ❑ LHD pp. 17–18 **Language & Sentence Skills Practice** ❑ OLL pp. 34–41 ❑ AL Literary Model pp. 42–43 ❑ AL Writing Application p. 44 **Lesson Plans for Language Development** ❑ pp. 274–275	**At Home: A Guide to Standards Mastery** ❑ Using Adjectives p. 27 ❑ **One-Stop Planner**
ASSESSMENT **Progress Assessment:** *Holt Handbook* ❑ Chapter 2 Test pp. 3–4		**One-Stop Planner** ❑ Test Generator
Chapter 3: Parts of Speech Overview ❑ Diagnostic Preview pp. 44–45	**Language & Sentence Skills Practice** ❑ Choices p. 45	❑ **One-Stop Planner**
	Spelling Lessons & Activities ❑ Unit 1 Review (Lesson 6) pp. 10–11	❑ **One-Stop Planner**

HOLT HANDBOOK

OPTIONAL *Daily Language Activities Transparencies*

Transparency 2   Proofreading Warm-ups
Transparency 27   Vocabulary: Deadwood Adjectives
Transparency 54   Analogies: Adjective : Quality
Transparency 72   Sentence Combining

Teaching Notes

GRADE 7: PUPIL'S EDITION AND HOLT HANDBOOK	STANDARDS-BASED COMPONENTS	SUPPORTING RESOURCES
HOLT LITERATURE & LANGUAGE ARTS		
Mini-Workshop 3: Writing a Descriptive Essay pp. 700–703 ❑ Practice & Apply p. 703	**Writing, Listening, & Speaking** ❑ Writing p. 122 ❑ Revising p. 123 **Lesson Plans for Language Development** ❑ p. 268	❑ **One-Stop Planner**
Progress Assessment: Writing, Listening, & Speaking ❑ Analytical Scale p. 66		❑ **One-Stop Planner**
HOLT HANDBOOK		
Chapter 3: Parts of Speech Overview, cont. ❑ The Verb pp. 45–53 ❑ The Adverb pp. 54–58 ❑ The Preposition pp. 58–61 ❑ The Conjunction pp. 62–65 ❑ The Interjection pp. 65–66 ❑ Determining Parts of Speech pp. 67–68 ❑ Chapter Review pp. 69–71 ❑ Writing Application p. 71	**Developmental Language & Sentence Skills** ❑ LHD pp. 19–28 **Language & Sentence Skills Practice** ❑ OLL pp. 46–64 ❑ AL Literary Model pp. 65–66 ❑ AL Writing Application p. 67 **Lesson Plans for Language Development** ❑ pp. 276–277	**At Home: A Guide to Standards Mastery** ❑ Using Adverbs p. 28 ❑ **One-Stop Planner**
ASSESSMENT **Progress Assessment:** *Holt Handbook* ❑ Chapter 3 Test pp. 5–6		**One-Stop Planner** ❑ Test Generator
	Spelling Lessons & Activities ❑ Lesson 7: Prefixes *en–* and *ex–* pp. 14–15	❑ **One-Stop Planner**
ASSESSMENT **Diagnostic & Summative Assessments** ❑ First-Quarter Test pp. 41–59		**One-Stop Planner** ❑ Test Generator

OPTIONAL   *Daily Language Activities Transparencies*

Transparency 3   Proofreading Warm-ups
Transparency 71   Analogies: Mixed

• **Red type** = Minimum Course of Study necessary to meet the California Standards
• **LHD** = Learners Having Difficulty (Benchmark/Strategic)   **OLL** = On-Level Learners   **AL** = Advanced Learners

Chapter 2 Overview
with Workshop 2, *Holt Handbook*

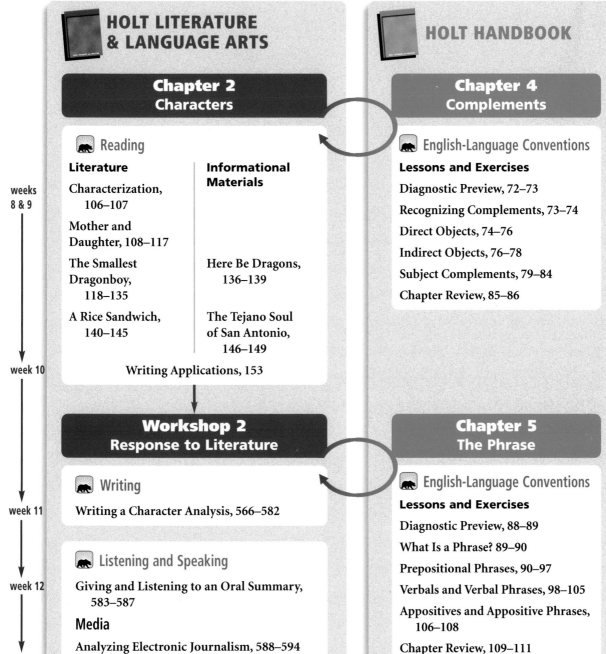

HOLT LITERATURE & LANGUAGE ARTS

GRADE 7: PUPIL'S EDITION AND HOLT HANDBOOK	STANDARDS–BASED COMPONENTS	SUPPORTING RESOURCES
Chapter 2: Characters ❑ Characterization pp. 106–107	**Interactive Reading** ❑ Strategy Launch and Practice Read pp. 47–56 **Lesson Plans for Language Development** ❑ pp. 39–40	❑ **One-Stop Planner** ❑ **One-Stop Planner**

Literature
❑ Mother and Daughter pp. 108–117
  ❑ Before You Read p. 108
  ❑ Focus On: questions and activities p. 116
  ❑ Vocabulary: Dictionaries Tell Stories p. 117
	Interactive Reading
	❑ p. 57
	Lesson Plans for Language Development
	❑ pp. 41–44, 55, 60
	Vocabulary Development
	❑ p. 9
		❑ **Audio CD Library**
		❑ **One-Stop Planner**

Progress Assessment: Reading, Vocabulary, & Literature ❑ Mother and Daughter pp. 32–34		**One-Stop Planner** ❑ Test Generator

Chapter 2: Characters, cont.
 	
Literature
❑ The Smallest Dragonboy pp. 118–135
  ❑ Before You Read p. 118
  ❑ Focus On: questions and activities p. 134
  ❑ Vocabulary: Recognizing Roots and Affixes p. 135
 	
Reading Matters
❑ Strategy Lesson 2: Understanding How Characters Affect Plot pp. 512–513
	Interactive Reading
	❑ p. 58
	Lesson Plans for Language Development
	❑ pp. 45–48, 56
	Vocabulary Development
	❑ pp. 10–11
		❑ **Audio CD Library**
		Fine Art Transparencies
		❑ Transparency 2
		At Home: A Guide to Standards Mastery
		❑ Improving Your Child's Spelling: Word Bases and Beyond p. 6
		❑ **One-Stop Planner**

Progress Assessment: Reading, Vocabulary, & Literature ❑ The Smallest Dragonboy pp. 35–37		**One-Stop Planner** ❑ Test Generator

• **Red type** = Minimum Course of Study necessary to meet the California Standards
• **LHD** = Learners Having Difficulty (Benchmark/Strategic) **OLL** = On-Level Learners **AL** = Advanced Learners

GRADE 7: PUPIL'S EDITION AND HOLT HANDBOOK	STANDARDS–BASED COMPONENTS	SUPPORTING RESOURCES
Chapter 4: Complements ❑ Diagnostic Preview pp. 72–73 ❑ Recognizing Complements pp. 73–74 ❑ Direct Objects pp. 74–76 ❑ Indirect Objects pp. 76–78	**Developmental Language & Sentence Skills** ❑ LHD pp. 29–32 **Language & Sentence Skills Practice** ❑ Choices p. 68 ❑ OLL pp. 69–73 **Lesson Plans for Language Development** ❑ p. 278	❑ **One-Stop Planner**
	Spelling Lessons & Activities ❑ Lesson 8: Prefixes *dis–* and *de–* pp. 16–17	❑ **One-Stop Planner**

OPTIONAL *Daily Language Activities Transparencies*

Transparency 22   Vocabulary: Frequently Confused Words
Transparency 46   Analogies: Part : Whole
Transparency 88   Critical Reading: Sentence Completions

Teaching Notes

HOLT HANDBOOK

GRADE 7: PUPIL'S EDITION AND HOLT HANDBOOK	STANDARDS-BASED COMPONENTS	SUPPORTING RESOURCES

Chapter 2: Characters, cont.
 	
Informational Material
❑ Here Be Dragons pp. 136–139
  ❑ Reading Informational Materials p. 136
  ❑ Focus On: questions and activities p. 139
	Interactive Reading
	❑ p. 59
	Lesson Plans for Language Development
	❑ pp. 49, 57, 61
		❑ **Audio CD Library**
		❑ **One-Stop Planner**

Progress Assessment: Reading, Vocabulary, & Literature ❑ Here Be Dragons pp. 38–39		**One-Stop Planner** ❑ Test Generator

Chapter 2: Characters, cont.
 	
Literature
❑ A Rice Sandwich pp. 140–145
  ❑ Before You Read p. 140
  ❑ Focus On: questions and activities p. 144
  ❑ Vocabulary: Borrowed Words p. 145
  ❑ Grammar Link: Avoiding Unclear Pronoun References p. 145
	Interactive Reading
	❑ p. 60
	Lesson Plans for Language Development
	❑ pp. 50–53, 58
		❑ **Audio CD Library**
		Visual Connections
		❑ Videocassette Segment 2
		❑ **One-Stop Planner**

Progress Assessment: Reading, Vocabulary, & Literature ❑ A Rice Sandwich pp. 40–42		**One-Stop Planner** ❑ Test Generator

Chapter 2: Characters, cont.
 	
Informational Material
❑ The Tejano Soul of San Antonio pp. 146–149
  ❑ Reading Informational Materials p. 146
  ❑ Focus On: questions p. 148
  ❑ Vocabulary: Using Word, Sentence, and Paragraph Clues p. 149
	Interactive Reading
	❑ p. 61
	Lesson Plans for Language Development
	❑ pp. 54, 59, 62
	Vocabulary Development
	❑ p. 12
		❑ **Audio CD Library**
		❑ **One-Stop Planner**

Progress Assessment: Reading, Vocabulary, & Literature ❑ The Tejano Soul of San Antonio pp. 43–44		**One-Stop Planner** ❑ Test Generator

HOLT LITERATURE & LANGUAGE ARTS

- **Red type** = Minimum Course of Study necessary to meet the California Standards
- **LHD** = Learners Having Difficulty (Benchmark/Strategic)   **OLL** = On-Level Learners   **AL** = Advanced Learners

Reading 1.2, 3.3
English-Language Conventions 1.0, 1.2, 1.3

	GRADE 7: PUPIL'S EDITION AND HOLT HANDBOOK	STANDARDS-BASED COMPONENTS	SUPPORTING RESOURCES
HOLT HANDBOOK	**Chapter 4: Complements,** cont. ❑ Subject Complements: Predicate Nominatives pp. 79–80 ❑ Subject Complements: Predicate Adjectives pp. 81, 82–84	**Developmental Language & Sentence Skills** ❑ LHD pp. 33–36 **Language & Sentence Skills Practice** ❑ OLL pp. 74–78 **Lesson Plans for Language Development** ❑ pp. 278–279	❑ **One-Stop Planner**
		Spelling Lessons & Activities ❑ Lesson 9: Places and People pp. 18–19	❑ **One-Stop Planner**

OPTIONAL *Daily Language Activities Transparencies*

Transparency 41	Vocabulary: Suffixes
Transparency 96	Critical Reading: Passage Completions
Transparency 104	Critical Reading: Passage Analysis

Standards Reinforcement: For students needing more help mastering Standard 3.3, teach "A Rice Sandwich."

Teaching Notes

GRADE 7: PUPIL'S EDITION AND HOLT HANDBOOK	STANDARDS–BASED COMPONENTS	SUPPORTING RESOURCES
	Interactive Reading ❑ OLL Four Selections pp. 62–66, 67 ❑ AL Top Ten Languages pp. 68–70, 71 ❑ AL Learning to Float pp. 72–80, 81	❑ **One-Stop Planner**
Chapter 2: Characters, cont. **Standards Review** ❑ Literary Response and Analysis pp. 150–151 ❑ Test Practice: Vocabulary Development p. 152	**Vocabulary Development** ❑ p. 13	❑ **One-Stop Planner**

ASSESSMENT
Progress Assessment: Reading, Vocabulary, & Literature
❑ Chapter Test
  ❑ Part A: Literary Response and Analysis pp. 45–46
  ❑ Part B: Reading Application pp. 47–51
		One-Stop Planner
		❑ Test Generator

Chapter 2: Characters, cont. ❑ Writing Applications: Response to Literature p. 153		
Workshop 2: Response to Literature **Writing a Character Analysis** ❑ Professional Model: A Response to Literature pp. 566–568 Prewriting pp. 568–573 ❑ Practice & Apply 1–3 pp. 571, 572, 573	**Writing, Listening, & Speaking** ❑ OLL Analyzing a Character p. 26 ❑ LHD Journal Warm-up: Character Analysis Transparency 8 ❑ LHD Prewriting: Character Analysis Writing Prompt Transparency 9 ❑ OLL Prewriting pp. 27, 29–30 ❑ Prewriting: Character Analysis Writing Prompts p. 28 **Lesson Plans for Language Development** ❑ p. 252	**At Home: A Guide to Standards Mastery** ❑ Helping Your Child Write a Character Analysis pp. 19–20 ❑ **One-Stop Planner**

HOLT LITERATURE & LANGUAGE ARTS

• **Red type** = Minimum Course of Study necessary to meet the California Standards
• **LHD** = Learners Having Difficulty (Benchmark/Strategic) **OLL** = On-Level Learners **AL** = Advanced Learners

GRADE 7: PUPIL'S EDITION AND HOLT HANDBOOK	STANDARDS-BASED COMPONENTS	SUPPORTING RESOURCES
Chapter 4: Complements, cont. ❑ Chapter Review pp. 85–86 ❑ Writing Application p. 87	**Language & Sentence Skills Practice** ❑ OLL pp. 79–81 ❑ AL Literary Model pp. 82–83 ❑ AL Writing Application p. 84	❑ **One-Stop Planner**
ASSESSMENT **Progress Assessment:** *Holt Handbook* ❑ Chapter 4 Test pp. 7–8		**One-Stop Planner** ❑ Test Generator
Chapter 5: The Phrase ❑ Diagnostic Preview pp. 88–89 ❑ What Is a Phrase? pp. 89–90 ❑ Prepositional Phrases pp. 90–91 ❑ Prepositional Phrases: Adjective Phrases pp. 92–94	**Developmental Language & Sentence Skills** ❑ LHD pp. 37–38, Exercises A and B pp. 39–40 **Language & Sentence Skills Practice** ❑ Choices p. 85 ❑ OLL pp. 86–88 **Lesson Plans for Language Development** ❑ pp. 280–281	❑ **One-Stop Planner**
	Spelling Lessons & Activities ❑ Lesson 10: Prefix *ad-* pp. 20–21	❑ **One-Stop Planner**

HOLT HANDBOOK

OPTIONAL *Daily Language Activities Transparencies*

Transparency 11   Proofreading Warm-ups
Transparency 55   Analogies: Mixed
Transparency 110   Critical Reading: Passage Analysis

Teaching Notes

HOLT LITERATURE & LANGUAGE ARTS

GRADE 7: PUPIL'S EDITION AND HOLT HANDBOOK	STANDARDS-BASED COMPONENTS	SUPPORTING RESOURCES
Workshop 2: Response to Literature, cont. **Writing a Character Analysis** Writing pp. 574–577 ❏ Practice & Apply 4 p. 574 Revising pp. 578–580 ❏ Practice & Apply 5 p. 580 Publishing pp. 581–582 ❏ Grammar Link: Punctuating Introductory Prepositional Phrases p. 581 ❏ Practice & Apply 6 p. 582	**Writing, Listening, & Speaking** ❏ LHD Think Sheet p. 31 ❏ LHD, OLL Writing p. 32 ❏ OLL Revising p. 33 ❏ AL Revising Practice p. 34 ❏ Revising: Evaluate Character Analyses p. 35 ❏ OLL Combining Sentences p. 36 ❏ OLL Proofreading p. 37 **Lesson Plans for Language Development** ❏ pp. 252–253 **Progress Assessment: Writing, Listening, & Speaking** [for help with revising and self-evaluation] ❏ Analytical Scale and Scoring Rubric pp. 36–38 ❏ General Scales and Sample Papers pp. 70–76, 86–94	❏ **One-Stop Planner**
ASSESSMENT **Progress Assessment: Writing, Listening, & Speaking** ❏ Writing Workshop 2 Test pp. 5–7 ❏ Analytical Scale and Scoring Rubric pp. 36–38 ❏ General Scales and Sample Papers pp. 70–76, 86–94		❏ **One-Stop Planner**
Workshop 2: Response to Literature, cont. **Giving and Listening to an Oral Summary** ❏ Choose an Article, Book, or Story p. 583 ❏ Read and Take Notes pp. 583–584	**Writing, Listening, & Speaking** ❏ Project-Planning Guide p. 40 **Lesson Plans for Language Development** ❏ p. 254	❏ **One-Stop Planner**

- **Red type** = Minimum Course of Study necessary to meet the California Standards
- **LHD** = Learners Having Difficulty (Benchmark/Strategic) **OLL** = On-Level Learners **AL** = Advanced Learners

GRADE 7: PUPIL'S EDITION AND HOLT HANDBOOK	STANDARDS-BASED COMPONENTS	SUPPORTING RESOURCES
Chapter 5: The Phrase, cont. ❑ Prepositional Phrases: Adverb Phrases pp. 94–97 ❑ Verbals and Verbal Phrases: The Participle pp. 98–100 ❑ Verbals and Verbal Phrases: The Participial Phrase pp. 100–102	**Developmental Language & Sentence Skills** ❑ LHD Exercise C, p. 40, 41–42 **Language & Sentence Skills Practice** ❑ OLL pp. 89–95 **Lesson Plans for Language Development** ❑ pp. 280–281	❑ **One-Stop Planner**
	Spelling Lessons & Activities ❑ Lesson 11: Adjective Suffixes pp. 22–23	❑ **One-Stop Planner**

(HOLT HANDBOOK)

OPTIONAL *Daily Language Activities Transparencies*

Transparency 16   Proofreading Warm-ups
Transparency 25   Vocabulary: Definitions
Transparency 73   Sentence Combining

Pacing Note: To help students state the main idea of an expository composition (Writing Standard 1.0), use The Parts of a Paragraph, pp. 683–686, in *Holt Literature & Language Arts.*

Teaching Notes

Week 12
Lesson Plan

Listening & Speaking 1.0, 1.1, 1.2, 1.4, 1.5, 1.6, 1.7, 1.8,
2.0, 2.2, 2.2a, 2.2b, 2.2c
English-Language Conventions 1.0, 1.2

GRADE 7: PUPIL'S EDITION AND HOLT HANDBOOK	STANDARDS-BASED COMPONENTS	SUPPORTING RESOURCES
Workshop 2: Response to Literature, cont. **Giving and Listening to an Oral Summary,** cont. ❑ Plan Your Presentation pp. 584–586 ❑ Deliver Your Presentation p. 586 ❑ Evaluate an Oral Summary pp. 586–587 ❑ Practice & Apply 7 p. 587	**Writing, Listening, & Speaking** ❑ LHD Think Sheet p. 41 ❑ OLL Think Sheet p. 42 ❑ AL Think Sheet p. 43 ❑ Evaluation Guide p. 44 **Lesson Plans for Language Development** ❑ p. 254	❑ **One-Stop Planner**
Progress Assessment: Writing, Listening, & Speaking ❑ Analytical Scale and Scoring Rubric pp. 39–41		❑ **One-Stop Planner**
Workshop 2: Response to Literature, cont. ❑ Standards Practice and Review p. 595		

	Writing, Listening, & Speaking
	❑ Choices p. 53
	    ❑ LHD Drama
	    ❑ OLL Speaking, Careers
	    ❑ AL Science
		❑ **One-Stop Planner**

Workshop 2: Response to Literature, cont. **Media Workshop: Analyzing Electronic Journalism** ❑ Textual Elements pp. 588–590 ❑ Visual Elements pp. 590–592 ❑ Audio Elements p. 593 ❑ Analysis of a News Story pp. 593–594 ❑ Practice & Apply 8 p. 594	**Writing, Listening, & Speaking** ❑ Project-Planning Guide p. 48 ❑ LHD Analyze Images Transparency 10 ❑ OLL Think Sheet p. 49 ❑ AL Think Sheet p. 50 ❑ Evaluation Guide p. 51 ❑ Video Think Sheet p. 52 **Lesson Plans for Language Development** ❑ p. 255	**Writing, Listening, & Speaking** ❑ Videocassette Segment 2 ❑ **One-Stop Planner**
Progress Assessment: Writing, Listening, & Speaking ❑ Analytical Scale and Scoring Rubric pp. 42–43		❑ **One-Stop Planner**

HOLT LITERATURE & LANGUAGE ARTS

• **Red type** = Minimum Course of Study necessary to meet the California Standards
• **LHD** = Learners Having Difficulty (Benchmark/Strategic) **OLL** = On-Level Learners **AL** = Advanced Learners

Week 12, continued
Lesson Plan

Listening & Speaking 1.0, 1.1, 1.2, 1.4, 1.5, 1.6, 1.7, 1.8,
2.0, 2.2, 2.2a, 2.2b, 2.2c
English-Language Conventions 1.0, 1.2

GRADE 7: PUPIL'S EDITION AND HOLT HANDBOOK	STANDARDS-BASED COMPONENTS	SUPPORTING RESOURCES
Chapter 5: The Phrase, cont. ❑ Verbals and Verbal Phrases: The Infinitive pp. 102–103 ❑ Verbals and Verbal Phrases: The Infinitive Phrase pp. 103–105 ❑ Appositives and Appositive Phrases pp. 106–108 ❑ Chapter Review pp. 109–111 ❑ Writing Application p. 111	**Developmental Language & Sentence Skills** ❑ LHD pp. 43–46 **Language & Sentence Skills Practice** ❑ OLL pp. 96–106 ❑ AL Literary Model pp. 107–108 ❑ AL Writing Application p. 109 **Lesson Plans for Language Development** ❑ p. 281	❑ **One-Stop Planner**
ASSESSMENT **Progress Assessment:** *Holt Handbook* ❑ Chapter 5 Test pp. 9–10		**One-Stop Planner** ❑ Test Generator
	Spelling Lessons & Activities ❑ Lesson 12: Spelling and Pronunciation pp. 24–25	❑ **One-Stop Planner**

OPTIONAL *Daily Language Activities Transparencies*

Transparency 13   Proofreading Warm-ups
Transparency 37   Vocabulary: Roots
Transparency 62   Analogies: Agent : Action
Transparency 80   Sentence Combining

Teaching Notes

HOLT HANDBOOK

Chapter 3 Overview
with Mini-Workshops 1 and 5, *Holt Handbook*

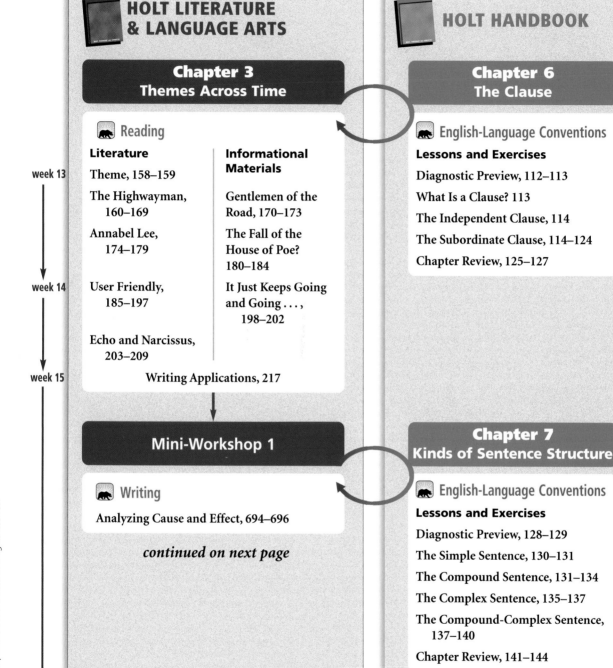

HOLT LITERATURE & LANGUAGE ARTS

Chapter 3
Themes Across Time

Reading

Literature

week 13

Theme, 158–159

The Highwayman, 160–169

Annabel Lee, 174–179

week 14

User Friendly, 185–197

Echo and Narcissus, 203–209

Informational Materials

Gentlemen of the Road, 170–173

The Fall of the House of Poe? 180–184

It Just Keeps Going and Going . . . , 198–202

week 15

Writing Applications, 217

Mini-Workshop 1

Writing

Analyzing Cause and Effect, 694–696

continued on next page

HOLT HANDBOOK

Chapter 6
The Clause

English-Language Conventions

Lessons and Exercises

Diagnostic Preview, 112–113

What Is a Clause? 113

The Independent Clause, 114

The Subordinate Clause, 114–124

Chapter Review, 125–127

Chapter 7
Kinds of Sentence Structure

English-Language Conventions

Lessons and Exercises

Diagnostic Preview, 128–129

The Simple Sentence, 130–131

The Compound Sentence, 131–134

The Complex Sentence, 135–137

The Compound-Complex Sentence, 137–140

Chapter Review, 141–144

continued on next page

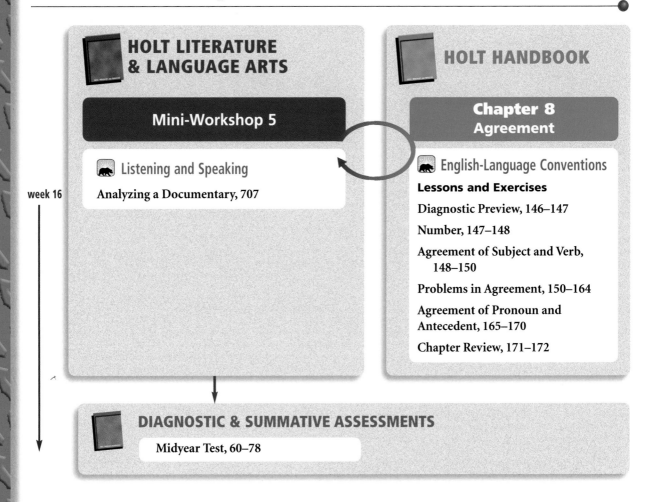

HOLT LITERATURE & LANGUAGE ARTS

Mini-Workshop 5

Listening and Speaking

Analyzing a Documentary, 707

week 16

HOLT HANDBOOK

**Chapter 8
Agreement**

English-Language Conventions

Lessons and Exercises

Diagnostic Preview, 146–147

Number, 147–148

Agreement of Subject and Verb, 148–150

Problems in Agreement, 150–164

Agreement of Pronoun and Antecedent, 165–170

Chapter Review, 171–172

DIAGNOSTIC & SUMMATIVE ASSESSMENTS

Midyear Test, 60–78

HOLT LITERATURE & LANGUAGE ARTS

GRADE 7: PUPIL'S EDITION AND HOLT HANDBOOK	STANDARDS-BASED COMPONENTS	SUPPORTING RESOURCES
Chapter 3: Themes Across Time ❑ Theme pp. 158–159 **Reading Matters** ❑ Strategy Lesson 3: Uncovering Theme pp. 514–515	**Interactive Reading** ❑ Strategy Launch and Practice Read pp. 83–89 **Lesson Plans for Language Development** ❑ pp. 63–64	❑ **One-Stop Planner** ❑ **One-Stop Planner**
Literature ❑ The Highwayman pp. 160–169 ❑ Before You Read p. 160 ❑ Focus On: questions and activities p. 168 ❑ Vocabulary: Similes and Metaphors p. 169	**Interactive Reading** ❑ p. 90 **Lesson Plans for Language Development** ❑ pp. 65–68, 84	❑ **Audio CD Library** **Fine Art Transparencies** ❑ Transparency 3 **Visual Connections** ❑ Videocassette Segment 3 ❑ **One-Stop Planner**
Progress Assessment: Reading, Vocabulary, & Literature ❑ The Highwayman pp. 52–54		**One-Stop Planner** ❑ Test Generator
Chapter 3: Themes Across Time, cont. **Informational Material** ❑ Gentlemen of the Road pp. 170–173 ❑ Reading Informational Materials p. 170 ❑ Focus On: questions p. 173	**Interactive Reading** ❑ p. 91 **Lesson Plans for Language Development** ❑ pp. 69, 85, 91	❑ **Audio CD Library** ❑ **One-Stop Planner**
Progress Assessment: Reading, Vocabulary, & Literature ❑ Gentlemen of the Road pp. 55–56		**One-Stop Planner** ❑ Test Generator
Chapter 3: Themes Across Time, cont. **Literature** ❑ Annabel Lee pp. 174–179 ❑ Before You Read p. 174 ❑ Focus On: questions and activities p. 178 ❑ Vocabulary: Using Analogies p. 179	**Interactive Reading** ❑ p. 92 **Lesson Plans for Language Development** ❑ pp. 70–73, 86	❑ **Audio CD Library** ❑ **One-Stop Planner**
Progress Assessment: Reading, Vocabulary, & Literature ❑ Annabel Lee pp. 57–59		**One-Stop Planner** ❑ Test Generator

• **Red type** = Minimum Course of Study necessary to meet the California Standards
• **LHD** = Learners Having Difficulty (Benchmark/Strategic)   **OLL** = On-Level Learners   **AL** = Advanced Learners

GRADE 7: PUPIL'S EDITION AND HOLT HANDBOOK	STANDARDS-BASED COMPONENTS	SUPPORTING RESOURCES

Chapter 3: Themes Across Time, cont.
 	
Informational Material
❑ Fall of the House of Poe? pp. 180–184
  ❑ Reading Informational Materials p. 180
  ❑ Focus On: questions and activities p. 183
  ❑ Vocabulary: Latin Roots p. 184
	Interactive Reading
	❑ p. 93
	
	Lesson Plans for Language Development
	❑ pp. 74, 87, 92
		❑ **Audio CD Library**
		❑ **One-Stop Planner**

Progress Assessment: Reading, Vocabulary, & Literature ❑ Fall of the House of Poe? pp. 60–61		**One-Stop Planner** ❑ Test Generator
Chapter 6: The Clause ❑ Diagnostic Preview pp. 112–113 ❑ What Is a Clause? p. 113 ❑ The Independent Clause p. 114 ❑ The Subordinate Clause pp. 114–117 ❑ The Subordinate Clause: The Adjective Clause pp. 117–119	**Developmental Language & Sentence Skills** ❑ LHD pp. 47–50 **Language & Sentence Skills Practice** ❑ Choices p. 110 ❑ OLL pp. 111–118 **Lesson Plans for Language Development** ❑ pp. 282–283	❑ **One-Stop Planner**
	Spelling Lessons & Activities ❑ Unit 2 Review (Lesson 13) pp. 26–27	❑ **One-Stop Planner**

HOLT LITERATURE & LANGUAGE ARTS

HOLT HANDBOOK

OPTIONAL   *Daily Language Activities Transparencies*

Transparency 26	Vocabulary: Suffixes
Transparency 57	Analogies: Part : Whole
Transparency 89	Critical Reading: Sentence Completions
Transparency 94	Critical Reading: Sentence Completions

Standards Reinforcement: If you anticipate that students will need further help in mastering Reading Standard 2.3, covered in "It Just Keeps Going and Going . . ." (Week 14), teach "Gentlemen of the Road" after you teach "The Highwayman."

Teaching Notes

HOLT LITERATURE & LANGUAGE ARTS

GRADE 7: PUPIL'S EDITION AND HOLT HANDBOOK	STANDARDS-BASED COMPONENTS	SUPPORTING RESOURCES

Chapter 3: Themes Across Time, cont.
 	
Literature
❑ User Friendly pp. 185–197
  ❑ Before You Read p. 185
  ❑ Focus On: questions and activities p. 196
  ❑ Vocabulary: Idioms p. 197
  ❑ Grammar Link: Pronouns Can Be Problems p. 197
	Interactive Reading
	❑ p. 94
	
	Lesson Plans for Language Development
	❑ pp. 75–78, 88
		❑ **Audio CD Library**
		
		At Home: A Guide to Standards Mastery
		❑ Expanding Your Child's Vocabulary: Idioms p. 9
		
		❑ **One-Stop Planner**

Progress Assessment: Reading, Vocabulary, & Literature ❑ User Friendly pp. 62–64		**One-Stop Planner** ❑ Test Generator

Chapter 3: Themes Across Time, cont.
 	
Informational Material
❑ It Just Keeps Going and Going . . . pp. 198–202
  ❑ Reading Informational Materials p. 198
  ❑ Focus On: questions and activities p. 201
  ❑ Vocabulary: Putting Analogies to Work p. 202
 	
Reading Matters
❑ Strategy Lesson 5: Identifying Cause and Effect pp. 518–519
	Interactive Reading
	❑ p. 95
	
	Lesson Plans for Language Development
	❑ pp. 79, 89, 93
		❑ **Audio CD Library**
		
		❑ **One-Stop Planner**

Progress Assessment: Reading, Vocabulary, & Literature ❑ It Just Keeps Going and Going . . . pp. 65–66		**One-Stop Planner** ❑ Test Generator

• **Red type** = Minimum Course of Study necessary to meet the California Standards
• **LHD** = Learners Having Difficulty (Benchmark/Strategic) **OLL** = On-Level Learners **AL** = Advanced Learners

HOLT LITERATURE & LANGUAGE ARTS

GRADE 7: PUPIL'S EDITION AND HOLT HANDBOOK	STANDARDS–BASED COMPONENTS	SUPPORTING RESOURCES

Chapter 3: Themes across Time, cont.
 	
 Literature
 ❑ Echo and Narcissus pp. 203–209
    ❑ Before You Read p. 203
    ❑ Focus On: questions and activities p. 208
    ❑ Vocabulary: Building Context Clues p. 209
    ❑ Grammar Link: Words Often Confused: *Its, It's and Your, You're* p. 209
	Interactive Reading
	 ❑ p. 96
	
	 Lesson Plans for Language Development
	 ❑ pp. 80–83, 90, 94
	
	 Vocabulary Development
	 ❑ p. 14
		❑ **Audio CD Library**
		
		 Fine Art Transparencies
		 ❑ Transparency 4
		
		 ❑ **One-Stop Planner**

Progress Assessment: Reading, Vocabulary, & Literature ❑ Echo and Narcissus pp. 67–69		**One-Stop Planner** ❑ Test Generator
	Interactive Reading ❑ LHD The Twelve Tasks of Heracles pp. 97–107, 108 ❑ OLL Words from the Myths pp. 109–114, 115 ❑ LHD Phaethon pp. 116–118, 119	❑ **One-Stop Planner**
Chapter 3: Themes Across Time, cont. **Standards Review** ❑ Literary Response and Analysis pp. 210–213 ❑ Reading Informational Materials pp. 214–215 ❑ Test Practice: Vocabulary Development p. 216	**Vocabulary Development** ❑ p. 15	❑ **One-Stop Planner**

ASSESSMENT
 	
 Progress Assessment: Reading, Vocabulary, & Literature
 ❑ Chapter Test
    ❑ Part A: Literary Response and Analysis pp. 70–71
    ❑ Part B: Reading Application pp. 72–77
		One-Stop Planner
		 ❑ Test Generator

GRADE 7: PUPIL'S EDITION AND HOLT HANDBOOK	STANDARDS-BASED COMPONENTS	SUPPORTING RESOURCES
Chapter 6: The Clause, cont. ❏ The Subordinate Clause: The Adverb Clause pp. 120–123, 123–124 ❏ Chapter Review pp. 125–127 ❏ Writing Application p. 127	**Developmental Language & Sentence Skills** ❏ LHD pp. 51–52 **Language & Sentence Skills Practice** ❏ OLL pp. 119–126 ❏ AL Literary Model pp. 127–128 ❏ AL Writing Application p. 129 **Lesson Plans for Language Development** ❏ pp. 282–283	❏ **One-Stop Planner**
ASSESSMENT **Progress Assessment:** *Holt Handbook* ❏ Chapter 6 Test pp. 11–12		**One-Stop Planner** ❏ Test Generator
Chapter 7: Kinds of Sentence Structure ❏ Diagnostic Preview pp. 128–129	**Language & Sentence Skills Practice** ❏ Choices p. 130	❏ **One-Stop Planner**
	Spelling Lessons & Activities ❏ Lesson 14: Noun Suffixes pp. 30–31	❏ **One-Stop Planner**

HOLT HANDBOOK

OPTIONAL *Daily Language Activities Transparencies*

Transparency 28	Vocabulary: Connotations
Transparency 59	Analogies: Word : Antonym
Transparency 97	Critical Reading: Passage Completions
Transparency 105	Critical Reading: Passage Analysis

• **Red type** = Minimum Course of Study necessary to meet the California Standards
• **LHD** = Learners Having Difficulty (Benchmark/Strategic) **OLL** = On-Level Learners **AL** = Advanced Learners

GRADE 7: PUPIL'S EDITION AND HOLT HANDBOOK	STANDARDS–BASED COMPONENTS	SUPPORTING RESOURCES
HOLT LITERATURE & LANGUAGE ARTS **Chapter 3: Themes Across Time,** cont. ❑ Writing Applications: Analyzing Cause and Effect p. 217		
Mini-Workshop 1: Analyzing Cause and Effect pp. 694–696 ❑ Practice & Apply p. 696	**Writing, Listening, & Speaking** ❑ Writing p. 118 ❑ Revising p. 119 **Lesson Plans for Language Development** ❑ p. 266	❑ **One-Stop Planner**
Progress Assessment: Writing, Listening, & Speaking ❑ Analytical Scale p. 64		❑ **One-Stop Planner**
HOLT HANDBOOK **Chapter 7: Kinds of Sentence Structure,** cont. ❑ The Simple Sentence pp. 130–131 ❑ The Compound Sentence pp. 131–134 ❑ The Complex Sentence pp. 135–137 ❑ The Compound-Complex Sentence pp. 137–138, 138–140 ❑ Chapter Review pp. 141–144 ❑ Writing Application pp. 144–145	**Developmental Language & Sentence Skills** ❑ LHD pp. 53–56 **Language & Sentence Skills Practice** ❑ OLL pp. 131–140 ❑ AL Literary Model pp. 141–142 ❑ AL Writing Application p. 143 **Lesson Plans for Language Development** ❑ pp. 284–285	❑ **One-Stop Planner**
ASSESSMENT **Progress Assessment:** *Holt Handbook* ❑ Chapter 7 Test pp. 13–14		**One-Stop Planner** ❑ Test Generator
Chapter 8: Agreement ❑ Diagnostic Preview pp. 146–147	**Language & Sentence Skills Practice** ❑ Choices p. 144	❑ **One-Stop Planner**

• **Red type** = Minimum Course of Study necessary to meet the California Standards
• **LHD** = Learners Having Difficulty (Benchmark/Strategic) **OLL** = On-Level Learners **AL** = Advanced Learners

40

GRADE 7: PUPIL'S EDITION AND HOLT HANDBOOK	STANDARDS–BASED COMPONENTS	SUPPORTING RESOURCES
	Spelling Lessons & Activities ❏ Lesson 15: Consonant and Syllable Patterns pp. 32–33	❏ **One-Stop Planner**

OPTIONAL *Daily Language Activities Transparencies*

Transparency 10   Proofreading Warm-ups
Transparency 43   Vocabulary: Roots
Transparency 60   Analogies: Mixed
Transparency 74   Sentence Combining

Pacing Note: To help students master Writing Standard 1.0, writing formal introductions and conclusions, teach Other Types of Paragraphs on p. 690 in *Holt Literature & Language Arts.*

Teaching Notes

	GRADE 7: PUPIL'S EDITION AND HOLT HANDBOOK	STANDARDS–BASED COMPONENTS	SUPPORTING RESOURCES
HOLT LITERATURE & LANGUAGE ARTS	**Mini-Workshop 5: Analyzing a Documentary** p. 707 ❑ Practice & Apply p. 707	**Writing, Listening, & Speaking** ❑ Think Sheet: Documentary p. 126 ❑ Evaluation Guide p. 127 **Lesson Plans for Language Development** ❑ p. 270	❑ **One-Stop Planner**
	Progress Assessment: Writing, Listening, & Speaking ❑ Analytical Scale p. 68		❑ **One-Stop Planner**
HOLT HANDBOOK	**Chapter 8: Agreement,** cont. ❑ Number pp. 147–148 ❑ Agreement of Subject and Verb pp. 148–150 ❑ Problems in Agreement pp. 150–164 ❑ Agreement of Pronoun and Antecedent pp. 165–169, 169–170 ❑ Chapter Review pp. 171–172 ❑ Writing Application pp. 172–173	**Developmental Language & Sentence Skills** ❑ LHD pp. 57–66 **Language & Sentence Skills Practice** ❑ OLL pp. 145–165 ❑ OLL, AL Proofreading Application p. 166 ❑ AL Literary Model pp. 167–168 ❑ AL Writing Application p. 169 **Lesson Plans for Language Development** ❑ pp. 286–287	❑ **One-Stop Planner**
	ASSESSMENT **Progress Assessment:** *Holt Handbook* ❑ Chapter 8 Test pp. 15–16		**One-Stop Planner** ❑ Test Generator

- **Red type** = Minimum Course of Study necessary to meet the California Standards
- **LHD** = Learners Having Difficulty (Benchmark/Strategic)   **OLL** = On-Level Learners   **AL** = Advanced Learners

GRADE 7: PUPIL'S EDITION AND HOLT HANDBOOK	STANDARDS–BASED COMPONENTS	SUPPORTING RESOURCES
	Spelling Lessons & Activities ❑ Lesson 16: Related Words pp. 34–35	❑ **One-Stop Planner**
ASSESSMENT **Diagnostic & Summative Assessments** ❑ Midyear Test pp. 60–78		**One-Stop Planner** ❑ Test Generator

OPTIONAL *Daily Language Activities Transparencies*

Transparency 14   Proofreading Warm-ups
Transparency 51   Analogies: Agent : Action
Transparency 81   Sentence Combining

Review: To reinforce mastery of English-Language Convention Standards 1.2 and 1.4, have students complete Exercises 8–13 on pp. 382–386, Correcting Common Errors, in the *Holt Handbook.*

Teaching Notes

Chapter 4 Overview
with Mini-Workshop 4, *Holt Handbook*

HOLT LITERATURE & LANGUAGE ARTS

Chapter 4
Point of View

📖 Reading

Literature

Point of View, 222–223

After Twenty Years, 224–231

Bargain, 236–249

Yeh-Shen, 250–256

Names/Nombres, 261–269

An Unforgettable Journey, 270–277

Elizabeth I, 282–295

Informational Materials

What's *Really* in a Name? 232–235

Mirror, Mirror, on the Wall, Do I See Myself As Others Do? 257–260

Exile Eyes, 278–281

Writing Applications, 301

week 17

weeks 18 & 19

week 20

Mini-Workshop 4

📖 Writing

Writing an Autobiographical Narrative, 704–706

HOLT HANDBOOK

Chapter 9
Using Verbs Correctly

📖 English-Language Conventions

Lessons and Exercises

Diagnostic Preview, 174–175

Principal Parts of Verbs, 175–186

Tense, 186–189

Active and Passive Voice, 189–190

Six Troublesome Verbs, 190–196

Chapter Review, 197–199

Chapter 10
Using Pronouns Correctly

📖 English-Language Conventions

Lessons and Exercises

Diagnostic Preview, 200–201

Case, 201–211

Special Pronoun Problems, 211–218

Chapter Review, 219–220

HOLT LITERATURE & LANGUAGE ARTS

GRADE 7: PUPIL'S EDITION AND HOLT HANDBOOK	STANDARDS–BASED COMPONENTS	SUPPORTING RESOURCES
Chapter 4: Point of View ❑ Point of View pp. 222–223	**Interactive Reading** ❑ Strategy Launch and Practice Read pp. 121–128 **Lesson Plans for Language Development** ❑ pp. 95–96	❑ **One-Stop Planner** **At Home: A Guide to Standards Mastery** ❑ Reinforcing Literary Concepts: Narrators and Points of View p. 7 ❑ **One-Stop Planner**

Literature
❑ After Twenty Years pp. 224–231
  ❑ Before You Read p. 224
  ❑ Focus On: questions and activities p. 230
  ❑ Vocabulary: Clarifying Word Meanings p. 231
  ❑ Grammar Link: End All End-Mark Errors p. 231
Reading Matters
❑ Strategy Lesson 4: Analyzing Point of View pp. 516–517
	Interactive Reading
	❑ p. 129
	
	Lesson Plans for Language Development
	❑ pp. 97–100, 122
	
	Vocabulary Development
	❑ pp. 16–17
		❑ **Audio CD Library**
		
		Fine Art Transparencies
		❑ Transparency 5
		
		❑ **One-Stop Planner**

Progress Assessment: Reading, Vocabulary, & Literature ❑ After Twenty Years pp. 78–80		**One-Stop Planner** ❑ Test Generator

Chapter 4: Point of View, cont.
 	
Informational Material
❑ What's *Really* in a Name? pp. 232–235
  ❑ Reading Informational Materials p. 232
  ❑ Focus On: questions p. 235
	Interactive Reading
	❑ p. 130
	
	Lesson Plans for Language Development
	❑ pp. 101, 123, 131
		❑ **Audio CD Library**
		
		❑ **One-Stop Planner**

Progress Assessment: Reading, Vocabulary, & Literature ❑ What's *Really* in a Name? pp. 81–82		**One-Stop Planner** ❑ Test Generator

- **Red type** = Minimum Course of Study necessary to meet the California Standards
- **LHD** = Learners Having Difficulty (Benchmark/Strategic) **OLL** = On-Level Learners **AL** = Advanced Learners

GRADE 7: PUPIL'S EDITION AND HOLT HANDBOOK	STANDARDS–BASED COMPONENTS	SUPPORTING RESOURCES

Chapter 4: Point of View, cont.
 	
Literature
❏ Bargain pp. 236–249
  ❏ Before You Read p. 236
  ❏ Focus On: questions and activities p. 248
  ❏ Vocabulary: Comprehension Strategies p. 249
	Interactive Reading
	❏ p. 131
	
	Lesson Plans for Language Development
	❏ pp. 102–105, 124, 132
		❏ **Audio CD Library**
		
		Fine Art Transparencies
		❏ Transparency 6
		
		❏ **One-Stop Planner**

Progress Assessment: Reading, Vocabulary, & Literature ❏ Bargain pp. 83–85		**One-Stop Planner** ❏ Test Generator
Chapter 9: Using Verbs Correctly ❏ Diagnostic Preview pp. 174–175 ❏ Principal Parts of Verbs pp. 175–186	**Developmental Language & Sentence Skills** ❏ LHD pp. 67–68 **Language & Sentence Skills Practice** ❏ Choices p. 170 ❏ OLL pp. 171–177 **Lesson Plans for Language Development** ❏ pp. 288–289	❏ **One-Stop Planner**
	Spelling Lessons & Activities ❏ Lesson 17: Latin Roots pp. 36–37	❏ **One-Stop Planner**

Side tabs: HOLT LIT & LANGUAGE ARTS · HOLT HANDBOOK

OPTIONAL   *Daily Language Activities Transparencies*

Transparency 34   Vocabulary: Definitions
Transparency 58   Analogies: Word : Synonym
Transparency 90   Critical Reading: Sentence Completions

Minimum Course of Study: Teach "An Unforgettable Journey" this week instead of during Week 18. See Week 18 for resources that accompany the story.

Teaching Notes

HOLT LITERATURE & LANGUAGE ARTS

GRADE 7: PUPIL'S EDITION AND HOLT HANDBOOK	STANDARDS-BASED COMPONENTS	SUPPORTING RESOURCES
Chapter 4: Point of View, cont. **Literature** ❑ Yeh–Shen pp. 250–256 　❑ Before You Read p. 250 　❑ Focus On: questions and activities p. 256	**Interactive Reading** ❑ p. 132 **Lesson Plans for Language Development** ❑ pp. 106–109, 125	❑ **Audio CD Library** ❑ **One-Stop Planner**
Progress Assessment: Reading, Vocabulary, & Literature ❑ Yeh–Shen pp. 86–88		**One-Stop Planner** ❑ Test Generator
Chapter 4: Point of View, cont. **Informational Material** ❑ Mirror, Mirror, on the Wall, Do I See Myself As Others Do? pp. 257–260 　❑ Reading Informational Materials p. 257 　❑ Focus On: questions p. 260	**Interactive Reading** ❑ p. 133 **Lesson Plans for Language Development** ❑ pp. 110, 126, 133	❑ **Audio CD Library** ❑ **One-Stop Planner**
Progress Assessment: Reading, Vocabulary, & Literature ❑ Mirror, Mirror, on the Wall, Do I See Myself As Others Do? pp. 89–90		**One-Stop Planner** ❑ Test Generator
Chapter 4: Point of View, cont. **Literature** ❑ Names/Nombres pp. 261–269 　❑ Before You Read p. 261 　❑ Focus On: questions and activities p. 267 　❑ Vocabulary: Clarifying Word Meanings p. 268 　❑ Grammar Link: Don't Leave Your Modifiers Dangling p. 269	**Interactive Reading** ❑ p. 134 **Lesson Plans for Language Development** ❑ pp. 111–114, 127, 134 **Vocabulary Development** ❑ p. 18	❑ **Audio CD Library** **Visual Connections** ❑ Videocassette Segment 4 ❑ **One-Stop Planner**
Progress Assessment: Reading, Vocabulary, & Literature ❑ Names/Nombres pp. 91–93		**One-Stop Planner** ❑ Test Generator

• **Red type** = Minimum Course of Study necessary to meet the California Standards
• **LHD** = Learners Having Difficulty (Benchmark/Strategic)　**OLL** = On-Level Learners　**AL** = Advanced Learners

GRADE 7: PUPIL'S EDITION AND HOLT HANDBOOK	STANDARDS-BASED COMPONENTS	SUPPORTING RESOURCES

HOLT LIT & LANGUAGE ARTS
 	
Chapter 4: Point of View, cont.
 	
Literature
❑ An Unforgettable Journey pp. 270–277
  ❑ Before You Read p. 270
  ❑ Focus On: questions and activities p. 276
  ❑ Vocabulary: Clarifying Meaning Through Contrast p. 277
	Interactive Reading
	❑ p. 135
	Lesson Plans for Language Development
	❑ pp. 115–118, 128
	Vocabulary Development
	❑ p. 19
		❑ **Audio CD Library**
		❑ **One-Stop Planner**

Progress Assessment: Reading, Vocabulary, & Literature ❑ An Unforgettable Journey pp. 94–96		**One-Stop Planner** ❑ Test Generator
HOLT HANDBOOK **Chapter 9: Using Verbs Correctly,** cont. ❑ Tense pp. 186–189 ❑ Active and Passive Voice pp. 189–190 ❑ Six Troublesome Verbs pp. 190–196 ❑ Chapter Review pp. 197–199 ❑ Writing Application p. 199	**Developmental Language & Sentence Skills** ❑ LHD pp. 69–72 **Language & Sentence Skills Practice** ❑ OLL pp. 178–188 ❑ OLL, AL Proofreading Application p. 189 ❑ AL Literary Model pp. 190–191 ❑ AL Writing Application p. 192	**At Home: A Guide to Standards Mastery** ❑ Understanding Voice p. 29 ❑ **One-Stop Planner**
ASSESSMENT **Progress Assessment:** *Holt Handbook* ❑ Chapter 9 Test pp. 17–18		**One-Stop Planner** ❑ Test Generator
	Spelling Lessons & Activities ❑ Lesson 18: Verb Suffixes pp. 38–39	❑ **One-Stop Planner**

OPTIONAL *Daily Language Activities Transparencies*

Transparency 5   Proofreading Warm-ups
Transparency 38   Vocabulary: Frequently Confused Words
Transparency 75   Sentence Combining
Transparency 98   Critical Reading: Passage Completions

Minimum Course of Study: Teach "Exile Eyes" this week instead of during Week 19. See Week 19 for resources that accompany "Exile Eyes."

Standards Reinforcement: For students needing further help mastering Standard 2.4, teach "Mirror, Mirror, on the Wall, Do I See Myself As Others Do?"

Review: To reinforce mastery of English-Language Convention Standard 1.4, have students complete Exercises 14–17 on pp. 386–389, Correcting Common Errors, in the *Holt Handbook.*

GRADE 7: PUPIL'S EDITION AND HOLT HANDBOOK	STANDARDS–BASED COMPONENTS	SUPPORTING RESOURCES

Chapter 4: Point of View, cont.
 	
Informational Material
❏ Exile Eyes pp. 278–281
  ❏ Reading Informational Materials p. 278
  ❏ Focus On: questions p. 281
	Interactive Reading
	❏ p. 136
	
	Lesson Plans for Language Development
	❏ pp. 119, 129, 135
		❏ **Audio CD Library**
		❏ **One-Stop Planner**

Progress Assessment: Reading, Vocabulary, & Literature ❏ Exile Eyes pp. 97–98		**One-Stop Planner** ❏ Test Generator

Chapter 4: Point of View, cont.
 	
Literature
❏ Elizabeth I pp. 282–295
  ❏ Before You Read pp. 282–283
  ❏ Focus On: questions and activities p. 294
  ❏ Vocabulary: Clarifying Word Meanings p. 295
	Interactive Reading
	❏ p. 137
	
	Lesson Plans for Language Development
	❏ pp. 120–121, 130, 136
	
	Vocabulary Development
	❏ p. 20
		❏ **Audio CD Library**
		❏ **One-Stop Planner**

Progress Assessment: Reading, Vocabulary, & Literature ❏ Elizabeth I pp. 99–101		**One-Stop Planner** ❏ Test Generator
	Interactive Reading ❏ OLL Thanksgiving with the Conners pp. 138–150, 151 ❏ OLL Miss Manners' Basic Training: Eating pp. 152–158, 159 ❏ OLL China's Little Ambassador pp. 160–166, 167	❏ **One-Stop Planner**

(sidebar) HOLT LITERATURE & LANGUAGE ARTS

- **Red type** = Minimum Course of Study necessary to meet the California Standards
- **LHD** = Learners Having Difficulty (Benchmark/Strategic) **OLL** = On-Level Learners **AL** = Advanced Learners

GRADE 7: PUPIL'S EDITION AND HOLT HANDBOOK	STANDARDS-BASED COMPONENTS	SUPPORTING RESOURCES
HOLT LITERATURE & LANGUAGE ARTS **Chapter 4: Point of View,** cont. **Standards Review** ❏ Literary Response and Analysis pp. 296–297 ❏ Reading Informational Materials pp. 298–299 ❏ Test Practice: Vocabulary Development p. 300	**Vocabulary Development** ❏ p. 21	❏ **One-Stop Planner**

ASSESSMENT
Progress Assessment: Reading, Vocabulary, & Literature
❏ Chapter Test
  ❏ Part A: Literary Response and Analysis pp. 102–103
  ❏ Part B: Reading Application pp. 104–108
		One-Stop Planner
		❏ Test Generator

HOLT HANDBOOK **Chapter 10: Using Pronouns Correctly** ❏ Diagnostic Preview pp. 200–201	**Language & Sentence Skills Practice** ❏ Choices p. 193	❏ **One-Stop Planner**
	Spelling Lessons & Activities ❏ Unit 3 Review (Lesson 19) pp. 40–41	❏ **One-Stop Planner**

OPTIONAL *Daily Language Activities Transparencies*

Transparency 6	Proofreading Warm-ups
Transparency 65	Analogies: Mixed
Transparency 82	Sentence Combining
Transparency 106	Critical Reading: Passage Analysis

Teaching Notes

GRADE 7: PUPIL'S EDITION AND HOLT HANDBOOK	STANDARDS–BASED COMPONENTS	SUPPORTING RESOURCES
Chapter 4: Point of View, cont. ❑ Writing Applications: Autobiographical Narrative p. 301		
Mini-Workshop 4: Writing an Autobiographical Narrative pp. 704–706 ❑ Practice & Apply p. 706	**Writing, Listening, & Speaking** ❑ Writing p. 124 ❑ Revising p. 125 **Lesson Plans for Language Development** ❑ p. 269	❑ **One-Stop Planner**
Progress Assessment: Writing, Listening, & Speaking ❑ Analytical Scale p. 67		❑ **One-Stop Planner**
Chapter 10: Using Pronouns Correctly, cont. ❑ Case pp. 201–211 ❑ Special Pronoun Problems pp. 211–217, 218 ❑ Chapter Review pp. 219–220 ❑ Writing Application p. 221	**Developmental Language & Sentence Skills** ❑ LHD pp. 73–80 **Language & Sentence Skills Practice** ❑ OLL pp. 194–209 ❑ OLL, AL Proofreading Application p. 210 ❑ AL Literary Model pp. 211–212 ❑ AL Writing Application p. 213 **Lesson Plans for Language Development** ❑ pp. 290–291	**At Home: A Guide to Standards Mastery** ❑ Identifying Unclear Pronoun References p. 30 ❑ **One-Stop Planner**
ASSESSMENT **Progress Assessment:** *Holt Handbook* ❑ Chapter 10 Test pp. 19–20		**One-Stop Planner** ❑ Test Generator
	Spelling Lessons & Activities ❑ Lesson 20: More Latin Roots pp. 44–45	❑ **One-Stop Planner**

Column labels at left: **HOLT LITERATURE & LANGUAGE ARTS** / **HOLT HANDBOOK**

OPTIONAL *Daily Language Activities Transparencies*

| Transparency 7 | Proofreading Warm-ups | Transparency 63 | Analogies: Agent : Acted Upon |
| Transparency 30 | Vocabulary: Synonyms | Transparency 86 | Sentence Combining |

Review: To reinforce mastery of English-Language Convention Standards 1.2 and 1.4, have students complete Exercises 18–20 on pp. 389–390, Correcting Common Errors, in the *Holt Handbook.*

• **Red type** = Minimum Course of Study necessary to meet the California Standards
• **LHD** = Learners Having Difficulty (Benchmark/Strategic)   **OLL** = On-Level Learners   **AL** = Advanced Learners

Chapter 5 Overview
with Workshop 3, *Holt Handbook*

 HOLT LITERATURE & LANGUAGE ARTS

Chapter 5
Worlds of Words

 Reading

Literature	Informational Materials
week 21 Reading Like a Wolf, 306–307	
Amigo Brothers, 308–319	Right Hook–Left Hook: The Boxing Controversy, 320–322
from Barrio Boy, 323–331	
week 22 Song of the Trees, 332–350	
Fish Cheeks, 351–356	
A Mason-Dixon Memory, 357–366	Buddies Bare Their Affection for Ill Classmate, 367–369
week 23 When the Earth Shakes, 370–379	
Painting with Words: The Elements of Poetry, 380–381	
I'm Nobody! 382–385	
I Am of the Earth *and* Early Song, 386–389	
The Sounds of Poetry, 390–391	
Madam and the Rent Man, 392–395	
The Runaway, 396–399	
maggie and milly and molly and may, 400–403	
week 24 Writing Applications, 407	

continued on next page

HOLT HANDBOOK

Chapter 11
Using Modifiers Correctly

English-Language Conventions

Lessons and Exercises

Diagnostic Preview, 222–223

What Is a Modifier? 223–224

Comparison of Adjectives and Adverbs, 224–228

Special Problems in Using Modifiers, 228–231

Double Negatives, 231–232

Placement of Modifiers, 232–240

Chapter Review, 241–243

continued on next page

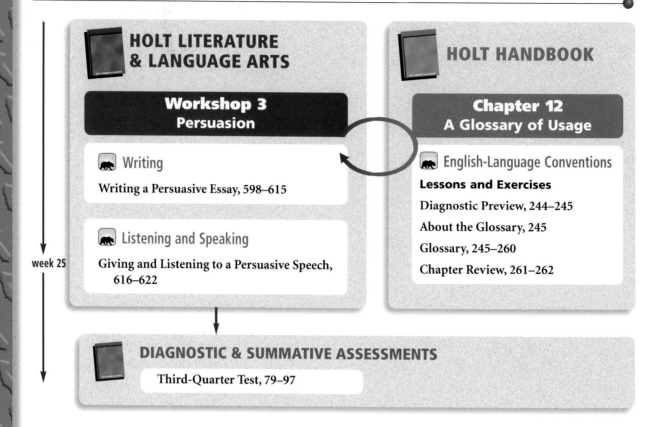

HOLT LITERATURE & LANGUAGE ARTS

Workshop 3
Persuasion

Writing

Writing a Persuasive Essay, 598–615

Listening and Speaking

Giving and Listening to a Persuasive Speech, 616–622

week 25

HOLT HANDBOOK

Chapter 12
A Glossary of Usage

English-Language Conventions

Lessons and Exercises

Diagnostic Preview, 244–245

About the Glossary, 245

Glossary, 245–260

Chapter Review, 261–262

DIAGNOSTIC & SUMMATIVE ASSESSMENTS

Third-Quarter Test, 79–97

HOLT LITERATURE & LANGUAGE ARTS

GRADE 7: PUPIL'S EDITION AND HOLT HANDBOOK	STANDARDS–BASED COMPONENTS	SUPPORTING RESOURCES
Chapter 5: Worlds of Words ❑ Reading Like a Wolf pp. 306–307	**Interactive Reading** ❑ Strategy Launch and Practice Read pp. 169–178 **Lesson Plans for Language Development** ❑ pp. 137–138	❑ **One-Stop Planner** ❑ **One-Stop Planner**

Literature
❑ Amigo Brothers pp. 308–319
  ❑ Before You Read p. 308
  ❑ Focus On: questions and activities p. 318
  ❑ Vocabulary: Clarifying Word Meanings p. 319
  ❑ Grammar Link: Punctuate Dialogue Correctly—And Punch Up Your Writing p. 319
	Interactive Reading
	❑ p. 179
	Lesson Plans for Language Development
	❑ pp. 139–142, 177
	Vocabulary Development
	❑ p. 22
		❑ **Audio CD Library**
		❑ **One-Stop Planner**

Progress Assessment: Reading, Vocabulary, & Literature ❑ Amigo Brothers pp. 109–111		**One-Stop Planner** ❑ Test Generator

Chapter 5: Worlds of Words, cont.
Informational Material
❑ Right Hook—Left Hook: The Boxing Controversy pp. 320–322
  ❑ Reading Informational Materials p. 320
  ❑ Focus On: questions and activity p. 322
	Interactive Reading
	❑ p. 180
	Lesson Plans for Language Development
	❑ pp. 143, 178, 191
		❑ **Audio CD Library**
		❑ **One-Stop Planner**

Progress Assessment: Reading, Vocabulary, & Literature ❑ Right Hook–Left Hook: The Boxing Controversy pp. 112–113		**One-Stop Planner** ❑ Test Generator

- **Red type** = Minimum Course of Study necessary to meet the California Standards
- **LHD** = Learners Having Difficulty (Benchmark/Strategic) **OLL** = On-Level Learners **AL** = Advanced Learners

	GRADE 7: PUPIL'S EDITION AND HOLT HANDBOOK	STANDARDS–BASED COMPONENTS	SUPPORTING RESOURCES
HOLT LITERATURE & LANGUAGE ARTS	**Chapter 5: Worlds of Words,** cont. **Literature** ❑ *from* Barrio Boy pp. 323–331 ❑ Before You Read p. 323 ❑ Focus On: questions and activities p. 329 ❑ Vocabulary: Clarifying Word Meanings p. 330 ❑ Grammar Link: Making the Most of Comparing Adjectives p. 331	**Interactive Reading** ❑ p. 181 **Lesson Plans for Language Development** ❑ pp. 144–147, 179, 192 **Vocabulary Development** ❑ p. 23	❑ **Audio CD Library** **Fine Art Transparencies** ❑ Transparency 7 **Visual Connections** ❑ Videocassette Segment 5 ❑ **One-Stop Planner**
	Progress Assessment: Reading, Vocabulary, & Literature ❑ *from* Barrio Boy pp. 114–116		**One-Stop Planner** ❑ Test Generator
HOLT HANDBOOK	**Chapter 11: Using Modifiers Correctly** ❑ Diagnostic Preview pp. 222–223 ❑ What Is a Modifier? pp. 223–224 ❑ Comparison of Adjectives and Adverbs pp. 224–228	**Developmental Language & Sentence Skills** ❑ LHD pp. 81–86 **Language & Sentence Skills Practice** ❑ Choices p. 214 ❑ OLL pp. 215–226 **Lesson Plans for Language Development** ❑ pp. 292–293	❑ **One-Stop Planner**
		Spelling Lessons & Activities ❑ Lesson 21: Unstressed Endings pp. 46–47	❑ **One-Stop Planner**

(OPTIONAL) *Daily Language Activities Transparencies*

Transparency 44   Vocabulary: Connotations
Transparency 48   Analogies: Word : Antonym
Transparency 91   Critical Reading: Sentence Completions

Teaching Notes

GRADE 7: PUPIL'S EDITION AND HOLT HANDBOOK	STANDARDS-BASED COMPONENTS	SUPPORTING RESOURCES

Chapter 5: Worlds of Words, cont.
 	
Literature
❑ Song of the Trees pp. 332–350
  ❑ Before You Read pp. 332–333
  ❑ Focus On: questions and activities p. 348
  ❑ Vocabulary: Connotations p. 349
  ❑ Grammar Link: All Modifiers! Places, Please! p. 350
	Interactive Reading
	❑ p. 182
	Lesson Plans for Language Development
	❑ pp. 148–151, 180, 193
	Vocabulary Development
	❑ p. 24
		❑ **Audio CD Library**
		Fine Art Transparencies
		❑ Transparency 8
		❑ **One-Stop Planner**

Progress Assessment: Reading, Vocabulary, & Literature ❑ Song of the Trees pp. 117–119		**One-Stop Planner** ❑ Test Generator

Chapter 5: Worlds of Words, cont.
 	
Literature
❑ Fish Cheeks pp. 351–356
  ❑ Before You Read p. 351
  ❑ Focus On: questions and activities p. 355
  ❑ Vocabulary: Analogies p. 356
	Interactive Reading
	❑ p. 183
	Lesson Plans for Language Development
	❑ pp. 152–155, 181, 194
	Vocabulary Development
	❑ p. 25
		❑ **Audio CD Library**
		Fine Art Transparencies
		❑ Transparency 9
		❑ **One-Stop Planner**

Progress Assessment: Reading, Vocabulary, & Literature ❑ Fish Cheeks pp. 120–122		**One-Stop Planner** ❑ Test Generator

Chapter 5: Worlds of Words, cont.
 	
Literature
❑ A Mason-Dixon Memory pp. 357–366
  ❑ Before You Read p. 357
  ❑ Focus On: questions and activities p. 364
  ❑ Vocabulary: Synonyms p. 365
  ❑ Grammar Link: Commas Make Sense of a Series p. 366
	Interactive Reading
	❑ p. 184
	Lesson Plans for Language Development
	❑ pp. 156–159, 182
	Vocabulary Development
	❑ p. 26
		❑ **Audio CD Library**
		Visual Connections
		❑ Videocassette Segment 6
		❑ **One-Stop Planner**

Progress Assessment: Reading, Vocabulary, & Literature ❑ A Mason-Dixon Memory pp. 123–124		**One-Stop Planner** ❑ Test Generator

HOLT LITERATURE & LANGUAGE ARTS

• **Red type** = Minimum Course of Study necessary to meet the California Standards
• **LHD** = Learners Having Difficulty (Benchmark/Strategic) **OLL** = On-Level Learners **AL** = Advanced Learners

GRADE 7: PUPIL'S EDITION AND HOLT HANDBOOK	STANDARDS-BASED COMPONENTS	SUPPORTING RESOURCES

Chapter 5: Worlds of Words, cont.
 	
Informational Material
❑ Buddies Bare Their Affection for Ill Classmate pp. 367–369
  ❑ Reading Informational Materials p. 367
  ❑ Focus On: questions and activities p. 369
	Interactive Reading
	❑ p. 185
	
	Lesson Plans for Language Development
	❑ pp. 160, 183, 195
		❑ **Audio CD Library**
		❑ **One-Stop Planner**

Progress Assessment: Reading, Vocabulary, & Literature ❑ Buddies Bare Their Affection for Ill Classmate pp. 125–126		**One-Stop Planner** ❑ Test Generator
Chapter 11: Using Modifiers Correctly, cont. ❑ Special Problems in Using Modifiers pp. 228–231 ❑ Double Negatives pp. 231–232 ❑ Placement of Modifiers pp. 232–239, 239–240	**Developmental Language & Sentence Skills** ❑ LHD pp. 87–90 **Language & Sentence Skills Practice** ❑ OLL pp. 227–235	**At Home: A Guide to Standards Mastery** ❑ Understanding Misplaced Modifiers p. 31 ❑ **One-Stop Planner**
	Spelling Lessons & Activities ❑ Lesson 22: More Latin Roots pp. 48–49	❑ **One-Stop Planner**

(left margin, first two rows) HOLT LITERATURE & LANGUAGE ARTS

(left margin, last two rows) HOLT HANDBOOK

OPTIONAL *Daily Language Activities Transparencies*
Transparency 21   Vocabulary: Synonyms
Transparency 47   Analogies: Word : Synonym
Transparency 99   Critical Reading: Passage Completions

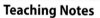

Teaching Notes

HOLT LITERATURE & LANGUAGE ARTS

GRADE 7: PUPIL'S EDITION AND HOLT HANDBOOK	STANDARDS-BASED COMPONENTS	SUPPORTING RESOURCES

Chapter 5: Worlds of Words, cont.
 	
Literature
❑ When the Earth Shakes pp. 370–379
  ❑ Before You Read p. 370
  ❑ Focus On: questions and activities p. 378
  ❑ Vocabulary: Clarifying Word Meanings p. 379
  ❑ Grammar Link: Formal and Informal English p. 379
	Interactive Reading
	❑ p. 186
	Lesson Plans for Language Development
	❑ pp. 161–164, 184, 196
	Vocabulary Development
	❑ p. 27
		❑ **Audio CD Library**
		❑ **One-Stop Planner**

Progress Assessment: Reading, Vocabulary, & Literature ❑ When the Earth Shakes pp. 127–129		**One-Stop Planner** ❑ Test Generator
Chapter 5: Worlds of Words, cont. ❑ Painting with Words: The Elements of Poetry pp. 380–381	**Interactive Reading** ❑ p. 187 **Lesson Plans for Language Development** ❑ pp. 165–166	❑ **One-Stop Planner**

Chapter 5: Worlds of Words, cont.
 	
Literature
❑ I'm Nobody! pp. 382–385
  ❑ Before You Read p. 382
  ❑ Focus On: questions and activities p. 385
	Lesson Plans for Language Development
	❑ pp. 167, 185
		❑ **Audio CD Library**
		❑ **One-Stop Planner**

Progress Assessment: Reading, Vocabulary, & Literature ❑ I'm Nobody! pp. 130–132		**One-Stop Planner** ❑ Test Generator

Chapter 5: Worlds of Words, cont.
 	
Literature
❑ I Am of the Earth *and* Early Song pp. 386–389
  ❑ Before You Read p. 386
  ❑ Focus On: questions and activities p. 389
	Lesson Plans for Language Development
	❑ pp. 168–170, 186–187, 197
		❑ **Audio CD Library**
		❑ **One-Stop Planner**

Progress Assessment: Reading, Vocabulary, & Literature ❑ I Am of the Earth *and* Early Song pp. 133–135		**One-Stop Planner** ❑ Test Generator

• **Red type** = Minimum Course of Study necessary to meet the California Standards
• **LHD** = Learners Having Difficulty (Benchmark/Strategic)   **OLL** = On-Level Learners   **AL** = Advanced Learners

GRADE 7: PUPIL'S EDITION AND HOLT HANDBOOK	STANDARDS–BASED COMPONENTS	SUPPORTING RESOURCES
Chapter 5: Worlds of Words, cont. ❏ The Sounds of Poetry pp. 390–391	**Lesson Plans for Language Development** ❏ pp. 171–172	❏ **One-Stop Planner**

Chapter 5: Worlds of Words, cont.
 	
Literature
❏ Madam and the Rent Man pp. 392–395
  ❏ Before You Read p. 392
  ❏ Focus On: questions and activities p. 395
	Lesson Plans for Language Development
	❏ pp. 173, 188
		❏ **Audio CD Library**
		Fine Art Transparencies
		❏ Transparency 10
		❏ **One-Stop Planner**

Progress Assessment: Reading, Vocabulary, & Literature ❏ Madam and the Rent Man pp. 136–138		**One-Stop Planner** ❏ Test Generator

Chapter 5: Worlds of Words, cont.
 	
Literature
❏ The Runaway pp. 396–399
  ❏ Before You Read p. 396
  ❏ Focus On: questions and activities p. 399
	Lesson Plans for Language Development
	❏ pp. 174, 189
		❏ **Audio CD Library**
		❏ **One-Stop Planner**

Progress Assessment: Reading, Vocabulary, & Literature ❏ The Runaway pp. 139–141		**One-Stop Planner** ❏ Test Generator

Chapter 5: Worlds of Words, cont.
 	
Literature
❏ maggie and milly and molly and may pp. 400–403
  ❏ Before You Read p. 400
  ❏ Focus On: questions and activities p. 403
	Lesson Plans for Language Development
	❏ pp. 175–176, 190, 198
		❏ **Audio CD Library**
		❏ **One-Stop Planner**

Progress Assessment: Reading, Vocabulary, & Literature ❏ maggie and milly and molly and may pp. 142–144		**One-Stop Planner** ❏ Test Generator
	Interactive Reading ❏ OLL *from* Volcano pp. 188–200, 201 ❏ AL Mexicans Resist Flight from "Friendly" Volcano pp. 202–208, 209 ❏ OLL Loo-Wit, the Fire-Keeper pp. 210–216, 217	❏ **One-Stop Planner**

HOLT LITERATURE & LANGUAGE ARTS

• **Red type** = Minimum Course of Study necessary to meet the California Standards
• **LHD** = Learners Having Difficulty (Benchmark/Strategic) **OLL** = On-Level Learners **AL** = Advanced Learners

GRADE 7: PUPIL'S EDITION AND HOLT HANDBOOK	STANDARDS-BASED COMPONENTS	SUPPORTING RESOURCES
Chapter 5: Worlds of Words, cont. **Standards Review** ❑ Literary Response and Analysis pp. 404–405 ❑ Test Practice: Vocabulary Development p. 406	**Vocabulary Development** ❑ p. 28	❑ **One–Stop Planner**

ASSESSMENT
 Progress Assessment: Reading, Vocabulary, & Literature
 ❑ Chapter Test
    ❑ Part A: Literary Response and Analysis pp. 145–146
    ❑ Part B: Reading Application pp. 147–151
		One-Stop Planner
		 ❑ Test Generator

Chapter 11: Using Modifiers Correctly, cont. ❑ Chapter Review pp. 241–243 ❑ Writing Application p. 243	**Language & Sentence Skills Practice** ❑ OLL pp. 236–239 ❑ OLL, AL Proofreading Application p. 240 ❑ AL Literary Model pp. 241–242 ❑ AL Writing Application p. 243	❑ **One–Stop Planner**
ASSESSMENT **Progress Assessment:** *Holt Handbook* ❑ Chapter 11 Test pp. 21–22		**One-Stop Planner** ❑ Test Generator
	Spelling Lessons & Activities ❑ Lesson 23: Words from French pp. 50–51	❑ **One-Stop Planner**

HOLT LITERATURE & LANGUAGE ARTS

HOLT HANDBOOK

OPTIONAL *Daily Language Activities Transparencies*

Transparency 8   Proofreading Warm-ups
Transparency 102   Critical Reading: Passage Completions
Transparency 107   Critical Reading: Passage Analysis

Standards Reinforcement: For students needing further help mastering Standard 3.1, teach "When the Earth Shakes."

Review: To reinforce mastery of English-Language Convention Standards 1.1 and 1.4, have students complete Exercises 21–24 on pp. 391–393, Correcting Common Errors, in the *Holt Handbook.*

GRADE 7: PUPIL'S EDITION AND HOLT HANDBOOK	STANDARDS-BASED COMPONENTS	SUPPORTING RESOURCES
Chapter 5: Worlds of Words, cont. ❑ Writing Applications: Persuasive Essay p. 407		
Workshop 3: Persuasion **Writing a Persuasive Essay** ❑ Professional Model: A Persuasive Essay pp. 598–601 Prewriting pp. 601–607 ❑ Practice & Apply 1–3, pp. 603, 604, 606 Writing pp. 608–610 ❑ Practice & Apply 4 p. 608 Revising pp. 611–613 ❑ Practice & Apply 5 p. 613	**Writing, Listening, & Speaking** ❑ LHD Journal Warm-up: Persuasive Essay Transparency 11 ❑ LHD Prewriting: Persuasive Essay Writing Prompt Transparency 12 ❑ Prewriting: Persuasive Essay Writing Prompts p. 56 ❑ OLL Prewriting pp. 55, 57–59 ❑ OLL Organization p. 60 ❑ LHD Think Sheet p. 61 ❑ LHD, OLL Writing p. 62 ❑ OLL Revising p. 63 ❑ AL Revising Practice p. 64 ❑ Revising: Evaluate Persuasive Essays p. 65 ❑ OLL Clichés p. 66 **Lesson Plans for Language Development** ❑ pp. 256–257 **Progress Assessment: Writing, Listening, & Speaking** [for help with revising and self-evaluation] ❑ Analytical Scale and Scoring Rubric pp. 44–46 ❑ General Scales and Sample Papers pp. 70–76, 95–103	**At Home: A Guide to Standards Mastery** ❑ Helping Your Child Plan a Persuasive Essay pp. 21–22 ❑ Practicing Consumer Skills with Your Child: Persuasive Techniques p. 10 ❑ **One-Stop Planner**

HOLT LITERATURE & LANGUAGE ARTS

• **Red type** = Minimum Course of Study necessary to meet the California Standards
• **LHD** = Learners Having Difficulty (Benchmark/Strategic) **OLL** = On-Level Learners **AL** = Advanced Learners

GRADE 7: PUPIL'S EDITION AND HOLT HANDBOOK	STANDARDS-BASED COMPONENTS	SUPPORTING RESOURCES
Chapter 12: A Glossary of Usage ❏ Diagnostic Preview pp. 244–245 ❏ About the Glossary p. 245 ❏ Glossary: *a, an* through *nowheres* pp. 245–254	**Developmental Language & Sentence Skills** ❏ LHD pp. 91–94 **Language & Sentence Skills Practice** ❏ Choices p. 244 ❏ OLL pp. 245–247 **Lesson Plans for Language Development** ❏ p. 294	❏ **One-Stop Planner**
	Spelling Lessons & Activities ❏ Lesson 24: Related Words pp. 52–53	❏ **One-Stop Planner**

OPTIONAL   *Daily Language Activities Transparencies*

Transparency 9   Proofreading Warm-ups
Transparency 40   Vocabulary: Frequently Confused Words
Transparency 64   Analogies: Action : Emotion
Transparency 76   Sentence Combining

Pacing Note: To help students master Writing Standards 1.0 and 1.1, use The Makings of a Good Paragraph on pp. 686-689 in *Holt Literature & Language Arts.*

Teaching Notes

Week 25
Lesson Plan

Writing 1.0, 2.0
Listening & Speaking 1.0, 1.1, 1.2,1.3, 1.4, 1.5, 1.6,1.7,
2.0, 2.4, 2.4a, 2.4b
English-Language Conventions 1.0, 1.4

GRADE 7: PUPIL'S EDITION AND HOLT HANDBOOK	STANDARDS–BASED COMPONENTS	SUPPORTING RESOURCES
Workshop 3: Persuasion, cont. **Writing a Persuasive Essay** Publishing pp. 614–615 ❑ Grammar Link: Using Comparatives p. 614 ❑ Practice & Apply 6 p. 615	**Writing, Listening, & Speaking** ❑ OLL Proofreading p. 67 **Lesson Plans for Language Development** ❑ p. 257	❑ **One-Stop Planner**
ASSESSMENT **Progress Assessment: Writing, Listening, & Speaking** ❑ Writing Workshop 3 Test pp. 8–10 ❑ Analytical Scale and Scoring Rubric pp. 44–46 ❑ General Scales and Sample Papers pp. 70–76, 95–103		❑ **One-Stop Planner**
Workshop 3: Persuasion, cont. **Giving and Listening to a Persuasive Speech** ❑ Adapt Your Persuasive Essay pp. 616–618 ❑ Deliver a Persuasive Speech pp. 618–619 ❑ Practice & Apply 7 p. 619 ❑ Listen to and Evaluate a Speech pp. 620–622 ❑ Practice & Apply 8 p. 622	**Writing, Listening, & Speaking** ❑ Project-Planning Guide p. 71 ❑ LHD Think Sheet p. 72 ❑ OLL Think Sheet p. 73 ❑ Evaluation Guide p. 74 ❑ Video Think Sheet pp. 75–76 **Lesson Plans for Language Development** ❑ p. 258	**Writing, Listening, & Speaking** ❑ Videocassette Segment 3 ❑ **One-Stop Planner**
Progress Assessment: Writing, Listening, & Speaking ❑ Analytical Scale and Scoring Rubric pp. 47–49		❑ **One-Stop Planner**
Workshop 3: Persuasion, cont. ❑ Standards Practice and Review p. 623		
	Writing, Listening, & Speaking ❑ Choices p. 77 ❑ LHD Careers ❑ OLL Writing, Art ❑ AL Social Studies	❑ **One-Stop Planner**

HOLT LITERATURE & LANGUAGE ARTS

• **Red type** = Minimum Course of Study necessary to meet the California Standards
• **LHD** = Learners Having Difficulty (Benchmark/Strategic) **OLL** = On-Level Learners **AL** = Advanced Learners

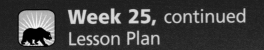

Week 25, continued
Lesson Plan

Writing 1.0, 2.0
Listening & Speaking 1.0, 1.1, 1.2, 1.3, 1.4, 1.5, 1.6, 1.7,
2.0, 2.4, 2.4a, 2.4b
English-Language Conventions 1.0, 1.4

HOLT HANDBOOK

GRADE 7: PUPIL'S EDITION AND HOLT HANDBOOK	STANDARDS–BASED COMPONENTS	SUPPORTING RESOURCES
Chapter 12: A Glossary of Usage, cont. ❏ Glossary: *of* through *your, you're* pp. 254–260, 260 ❏ Chapter Review pp. 261–262 ❏ Writing Application p. 263	**Developmental Language & Sentence Skills** ❏ LHD pp. 95–96 **Language & Sentence Skills Practice** ❏ OLL pp. 248–253 ❏ OLL, AL Proofreading p. 253 ❏ AL Literary Model pp. 254–255 ❏ AL Writing Application p. 256 **Lesson Plans for Language Development** ❏ pp. 294–295	❏ **One-Stop Planner**
ASSESSMENT **Progress Assessment:** *Holt Handbook* ❏ Chapter 12 Test pp. 23–24		**One-Stop Planner** ❏ Test Generator
	Spelling Lessons & Activities ❏ Lesson 25: More Related Words pp. 54–55	❏ **One-Stop Planner**
ASSESSMENT **Diagnostic & Summative Assessments** ❏ Third-Quarter Test pp. 79–97		**One-Stop Planner** ❏ Test Generator

OPTIONAL *Daily Language Activities Transparencies*

Transparency 12   Proofreading Warm-ups
Transparency 68   Analogies: Mixed
Transparency 83   Sentence Combining

Review: To reinforce mastery of English-Language Convention Standard 1.4, have students complete Exercises 25–27 on pp. 393–395, Correcting Common Errors, in the *Holt Handbook.*

Teaching Notes

Chapter 6 Overview

with Workshop 4, Mini-Workshop 2, *Holt Handbook*

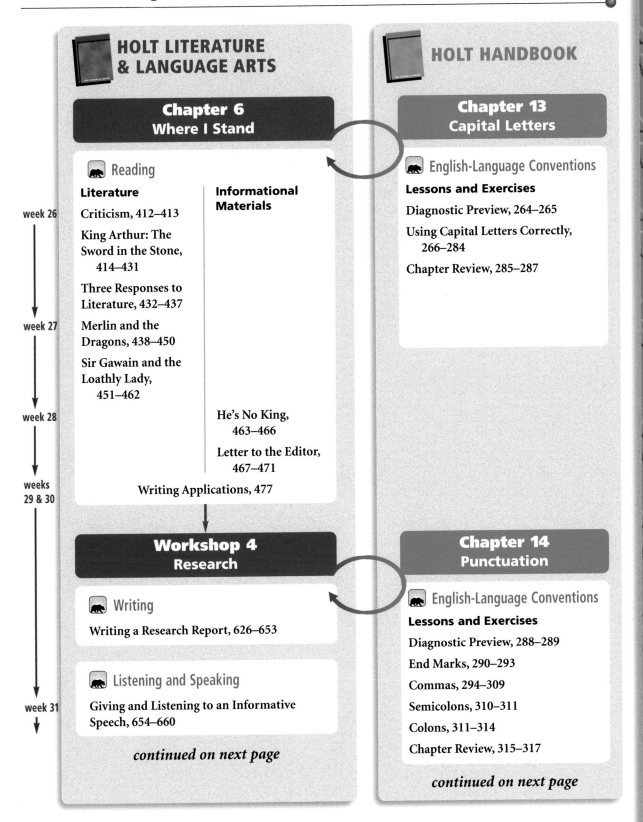

HOLT LITERATURE & LANGUAGE ARTS

Chapter 6
Where I Stand

Reading

Literature

Criticism, 412–413

King Arthur: The Sword in the Stone, 414–431

Three Responses to Literature, 432–437

Merlin and the Dragons, 438–450

Sir Gawain and the Loathly Lady, 451–462

Informational Materials

He's No King, 463–466

Letter to the Editor, 467–471

Writing Applications, 477

Workshop 4
Research

Writing

Writing a Research Report, 626–653

Listening and Speaking

Giving and Listening to an Informative Speech, 654–660

continued on next page

week 26

week 27

week 28

weeks 29 & 30

week 31

HOLT HANDBOOK

Chapter 13
Capital Letters

English-Language Conventions

Lessons and Exercises

Diagnostic Preview, 264–265

Using Capital Letters Correctly, 266–284

Chapter Review, 285–287

Chapter 14
Punctuation

English-Language Conventions

Lessons and Exercises

Diagnostic Preview, 288–289

End Marks, 290–293

Commas, 294–309

Semicolons, 310–311

Colons, 311–314

Chapter Review, 315–317

continued on next page

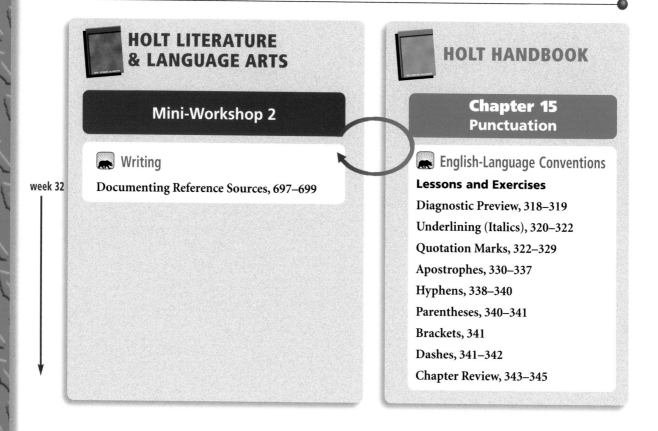

HOLT LITERATURE & LANGUAGE ARTS

Mini-Workshop 2

🐻 Writing

week 32

HOLT HANDBOOK

Chapter 15
Punctuation

🐻 English-Language Conventions

HOLT LITERATURE & LANGUAGE ARTS

GRADE 7: PUPIL'S EDITION AND HOLT HANDBOOK	STANDARDS–BASED COMPONENTS	SUPPORTING RESOURCES
Chapter 6: Where I Stand ❑ Criticism pp. 412–413	**Interactive Reading** ❑ Strategy Launch and Practice Read pp. 219–232 **Lesson Plans for Language Development** ❑ pp. 199–200	❑ **One-Stop Planner** ❑ **One-Stop Planner**

Literature
❑ King Arthur: The Sword in the Stone pp. 414–431
  ❑ Before You Read p. 414
  ❑ Focus On: questions and activities p. 430
  ❑ Vocabulary: Where Do Words Come From? p. 431
	Interactive Reading
	❑ p. 233
	Lesson Plans for Language Development
	❑ pp. 201–204, 215, 221
	Vocabulary Development
	❑ p. 29
		❑ **Audio CD Library**
		Fine Art Transparencies
		❑ Transparency 11
		❑ **One-Stop Planner**

Progress Assessment: Reading, Vocabulary, & Literature ❑ King Arthur: The Sword in the Stone pp. 152–154		**One-Stop Planner** ❑ Test Generator

Chapter 6: Where I Stand, cont.
Literature
❑ Three Responses to Literature pp. 432–437
  ❑ Before You Read p. 432
  ❑ Focus On: questions p. 436
  ❑ Vocabulary: The Useful Prefix p. 437
	Interactive Reading
	❑ p. 234
	Lesson Plans for Language Development
	❑ pp. 205, 216, 222
		❑ **One-Stop Planner**

Progress Assessment: Reading, Vocabulary, & Literature ❑ Three Responses to Literature pp. 155–156		**One-Stop Planner** ❑ Test Generator

· **Red type** = Minimum Course of Study necessary to meet the California Standards
· **LHD** = Learners Having Difficulty (Benchmark/Strategic)   **OLL** = On-Level Learners   **AL** = Advanced Learners

GRADE 7: PUPIL'S EDITION AND HOLT HANDBOOK	STANDARDS-BASED COMPONENTS	SUPPORTING RESOURCES
Chapter 13: Capital Letters ❑ Diagnostic Preview pp. 264–265 ❑ Using Capital Letters Correctly pp. 266–270	**Developmental Language & Sentence Skills** ❑ LHD pp. 97–102 **Language & Sentence Skills Practice** ❑ Choices p. 257 ❑ OLL pp. 258–260	❑ **One-Stop Planner**
	Spelling Lessons & Activities ❑ Unit 4 Review (Lesson 26) pp. 56–57	❑ **One-Stop Planner**

HOLT HANDBOOK

OPTIONAL   *Daily Language Activities Transparencies*

Transparency 24   Vocabulary: Prefixes
Transparency 92   Critical Reading: Sentence Completions

Teaching Notes

GRADE 7: PUPIL'S EDITION AND HOLT HANDBOOK	STANDARDS–BASED COMPONENTS	SUPPORTING RESOURCES

Chapter 6: Where I Stand, cont.
 	
Literature
❑ Merlin and the Dragons pp. 438–450
   ❑ Before You Read p. 438
   ❑ Focus On: questions and activities p. 449
   ❑ Vocabulary: Prefixes and Suffixes p. 450
	Interactive Reading
	❑ p. 235
	Lesson Plans for Language Development
	❑ pp. 206–208, 217, 223
	Vocabulary Development
	❑ p. 30
		❑ **Audio CD Library**
		Fine Art Transparencies
		❑ Transparency 12
		❑ **One-Stop Planner**

Progress Assessment: Reading, Vocabulary, & Literature ❑ Merlin and the Dragons pp. 157–159		❑ **One-Stop Planner** ❑ Test Generator

Chapter 6: Where I Stand, cont.
 	
Literature
❑ Sir Gawain and the Loathly Lady pp. 451–462
   ❑ Before You Read p. 451
   ❑ Focus On: questions and activities p. 460
   ❑ Vocabulary: The French Influence p. 461
   ❑ Grammar Link: Words Often Confused p. 462
	Interactive Reading
	❑ p. 236
	Lesson Plans for Language Development
	❑ pp. 209–212, 218, 224
	Vocabulary Development
	❑ p. 31
		❑ **Audio CD Library**
		❑ **One-Stop Planner**

Progress Assessment: Reading, Vocabulary, & Literature ❑ Sir Gawain and the Loathly Lady pp. 160–162		❑ **One-Stop Planner** ❑ Test Generator
Chapter 13: Capital Letters, cont. ❑ Using Capital Letters Correctly pp. 271–281, 281–284	**Developmental Language & Sentence Skills** ❑ LHD pp. 103–108 **Language & Sentence Skills Practice** ❑ OLL pp. 261–273 **Lesson Plans for Language Development** ❑ pp. 296–297	**At Home: A Guide to Standards Mastery** ❑ Capitalizing Proper Adjectives p. 32 ❑ **One-Stop Planner**

HOLT LITERATURE & LANGUAGE ARTS

HOLT HANDBOOK

• **Red type** = Minimum Course of Study necessary to meet the California Standards
• **LHD** = Learners Having Difficulty (Benchmark/Strategic) **OLL** = On-Level Learners **AL** = Advanced Learners

GRADE 7: PUPIL'S EDITION AND HOLT HANDBOOK	STANDARDS-BASED COMPONENTS	SUPPORTING RESOURCES
	Spelling Lessons & Activities ❑ Lesson 27: Greek Word Parts pp. 60–61	❑ **One-Stop Planner**

OPTIONAL *Daily Language Activities Transparencies*

Transparency 32   Vocabulary: Connotations
Transparency 61   Analogies: Noun : Quality
Transparency 100   Critical Reading: Passage Completions

Teaching Notes

GRADE 7: PUPIL'S EDITION AND HOLT HANDBOOK	STANDARDS-BASED COMPONENTS	SUPPORTING RESOURCES

Chapter 6: Where I Stand, cont.
 	
 Informational Material
 ❑ He's No King pp. 463–466
   ❑ Reading Informational Materials p. 463
   ❑ Focus On: questions p. 465
   ❑ Vocabulary: It's Greek to Me p. 466
 	
 Reading Matters
 ❑ Strategy Lesson 6: Latin and Greek Roots and Affixes pp. 520–523
	Interactive Reading
	 ❑ p. 237
	
	 Lesson Plans for Language Development
	 ❑ pp. 213, 219
		❑ **Audio CD Library**
		 ❑ **One-Stop Planner**

Progress Assessment: Reading, Vocabulary, & Literature ❑ He's No King pp. 163–164		**One-Stop Planner** ❑ Test Generator

Chapter 6: Where I Stand, cont.
 	
 Informational Material
 ❑ Letter to the Editor pp. 467–471
   ❑ Reading Informational Materials pp. 467–468
   ❑ Focus On: questions pp. 470–471
	Interactive Reading
	 ❑ p. 238
	
	 Lesson Plans for Language Development
	 ❑ pp. 214, 220, 225
		❑ **Audio CD Library**
		 ❑ **One-Stop Planner**

Progress Assessment: Reading, Vocabulary, & Literature ❑ Letter to the Editor pp. 165–166		**One-Stop Planner** ❑ Test Generator
	Interactive Reading ❑ OLL The Changing of the Shrew *and* Magical Merlin pp. 239–253 ❑ OLL In Search of King Arthur pp. 254–259 ❑ LHD Camelot pp. 260–263	❑ **One-Stop Planner**
Chapter 6: Where I Stand, cont. **Standards Review** ❑ Literary Response and Analysis pp. 472–473 ❑ Reading Informational Materials pp. 474–475 ❑ Test Practice: Vocabulary Development p. 476	**Vocabulary Development** ❑ p. 32	❑ **One-Stop Planner**

GRADE 7: PUPIL'S EDITION AND HOLT HANDBOOK	STANDARDS–BASED COMPONENTS	SUPPORTING RESOURCES
HOLT LIT & LANGUAGE ARTS **ASSESSMENT** **Progress Assessment: Reading, Vocabulary, & Literature** ❑ Chapter Test ❑ Part A: Literary Response and Analysis pp. 167–168 ❑ Part B: Reading Application pp. 169–172		**One-Stop Planner** ❑ Test Generator
HOLT HANDBOOK **Chapter 13: Capital Letters,** cont. ❑ Chapter Review pp. 285–287 ❑ Writing Application p. 287	**Language & Sentence Skills Practice** ❑ OLL pp. 273–275 ❑ OLL, AL Proofreading Application p. 276 ❑ AL Literary Model pp. 277–278 ❑ AL Writing Application p. 279	❑ **One-Stop Planner**
ASSESSMENT **Progress Assessment:** *Holt Handbook* ❑ Chapter 13 Test pp. 25–26		**One-Stop Planner** ❑ Test Generator
	Spelling Lessons & Activities ❑ Lesson 28: Number Prefixes pp. 62–63	❑ **One-Stop Planner**

OPTIONAL *Daily Language Activities Transparencies*

Transparency 36   Vocabulary: Deadwood Adjectives
Transparency 66   Analogies: Adjective : Quality
Transparency 108 Critical Reading: Passage Analysis

Standards Reinforcement: For students needing further help mastering Reading Standard 2.6, teach either "He's No King" or "Letter to the Editor."

Review: To reinforce mastery of English-Language Convention Standard 1.6, have students complete Exercises 28–29 on pp. 400–401, Correcting Common Errors, in the *Holt Handbook.*

GRADE 7: PUPIL'S EDITION AND HOLT HANDBOOK	STANDARDS–BASED COMPONENTS	SUPPORTING RESOURCES
Chapter 6: Where I Stand, cont. ❑ Writing Applications: Research Report p. 477		
Workshop 4: Research **Writing a Research Report** ❑ Professional Model: A Research Report pp. 626–630 Prewriting pp. 630–633 ❑ Practice & Apply 1–2 pp. 631, 633	**Writing, Listening, & Speaking** ❑ Prewriting: Research Report Writing Prompts p. 79 ❑ LHD Journal Warm-up: Research Report Transparency 13 ❑ OLL Prewriting pp. 80–81 **Lesson Plans for Language Development** ❑ p. 259	**At Home: A Guide to Standards Mastery** ❑ Helping Your Child Plan a Research Report pp. 23–24 ❑ **One-Stop Planner**
Chapter 14: Punctuation ❑ Diagnostic Preview pp. 288–289 ❑ End Marks pp. 290–293 ❑ Commas pp. 294–297 ❑ Commas: Compound Sentences pp. 297–299	**Developmental Language & Sentence Skills** ❑ LHD pp. 109–110 **Language & Sentence Skills Practice** ❑ Choices p. 280 ❑ OLL pp. 281–285 **Lesson Plans for Language Development** ❑ p. 298	❑ **One-Stop Planner**
	Spelling Lessons & Activities ❑ Lesson 29: Spelling and Pronunciation pp. 64–65	❑ **One-Stop Planner**

Side labels: **HOLT LITERATURE & LANGUAGE ARTS** / **HOLT HANDBOOK**

OPTIONAL *Daily Language Activities Transparencies*

Transparency 15   Proofreading Warm-ups
Transparency 45   Vocabulary: Frequently Confused Words

Pacing Note: To help students support main ideas with sensory details, facts, and examples (Writing Standards 1.0 and 1.2), use Supporting Sentences on pp. 685–686 in *Holt Literature & Language Arts.*

• **Red type** = Minimum Course of Study necessary to meet the California Standards
• **LHD** = Learners Having Difficulty (Benchmark/Strategic)   **OLL** = On-Level Learners   **AL** = Advanced Learners

GRADE 7: PUPIL'S EDITION AND HOLT HANDBOOK	STANDARDS–BASED COMPONENTS	SUPPORTING RESOURCES
Workshop 4: Research, cont. **Writing a Research Report** Prewriting pp. 633–641 ❑ Practice & Apply 3–7, pp. 635, 638, 639, 640, 641 Writing pp. 642–648 ❑ Practice & Apply 8 p. 648 Revising pp. 649–651 ❑ Practice & Apply 9 p. 651	**Writing, Listening, & Speaking** ❑ LHD Prewriting: Research Report Writing Prompt Transparency 14 ❑ OLL Prewriting pp. 82, 84–87 ❑ OLL Evaluating Sources p. 83 ❑ LHD Think Sheet p. 88 ❑ LHD, OLL Writing p. 89 ❑ OLL Revising p. 90 ❑ AL Revising Practice p. 91 ❑ Revising: Evaluate Research Reports p. 92 ❑ OLL Varying Sentence Beginnings p. 93 **Lesson Plans for Language Development** ❑ pp. 259–260 **Progress Assessment: Writing, Listening, & Speaking** [for help with revising and self-evaluation] ❑ Analytical Scale and Scoring Rubric pp. 50–52	❑ **One-Stop Planner**

HOLT LITERATURE & LANGUAGE ARTS

• **Red type** = Minimum Course of Study necessary to meet the California Standards
• **LHD** = Learners Having Difficulty (Benchmark/Strategic)   **OLL** = On-Level Learners   **AL** = Advanced Learners

GRADE 7: PUPIL'S EDITION AND HOLT HANDBOOK	STANDARDS–BASED COMPONENTS	SUPPORTING RESOURCES
Chapter 14: Punctuation, cont. ❑ Commas: Interrupters pp. 299–304 ❑ Commas: Introductory Words, Phrases, and Clauses pp. 305–306 ❑ Commas: Conventional Situations pp. 306–309 ❑ Semicolons pp. 310–311 ❑ Colons pp. 311–314 ❑ Chapter Review pp. 315–317	**Developmental Language & Sentence Skills** ❑ LHD pp. 111–114 **Language & Sentence Skills Practice** ❑ OLL pp. 286–300 **Lesson Plans for Language Development** ❑ pp. 298–299	❑ **One-Stop Planner**
ASSESSMENT **Progress Assessment:** *Holt Handbook* ❑ Chapter 14 Test pp. 27–28		**One-Stop Planner** ❑ Test Generator
	Spelling Lessons & Activities ❑ Lesson 30: Clipped Words pp. 66–67	❑ **One-Stop Planner**

OPTIONAL   *Daily Language Activities Transparencies*

Transparency 17   Proofreading Warm-ups
Transparency 77   Sentence Combining

Review: To reinforce mastery of English-Language Convention Standards 1.4 and 1.5, have students complete Exercises 30–32 on pp. 401–403, Correcting Common Errors, in the *Holt Handbook.*

Teaching Notes

Writing 1.6, 2.0
Listening and Speaking 1.0, 1.1, 1.2, 1.4, 1.5, 1.6, 1.7, 2.0, 2.3a, 2.3b, 2.3c, 2.3d
English-Language Conventions 1.0, 1.4, 1.5

GRADE 7: PUPIL'S EDITION AND HOLT HANDBOOK	STANDARDS–BASED COMPONENTS	SUPPORTING RESOURCES
Workshop 4: Research, cont. **Writing a Research Report** Publishing pp. 652–653 ❑ Grammar Link: Title Treatments p. 652 ❑ Practice & Apply 10 p. 653	**Writing, Listening, & Speaking** ❑ OLL Proofreading p. 94 **Lesson Plans for Language Development** ❑ p. 260	❑ **One-Stop Planner**
ASSESSMENT **Progress Assessment: Writing, Listening, & Speaking** ❑ Writing Workshop 4 Test pp. 11–13 ❑ Analytical Scale and Scoring Rubric pp. 50–52		❑ **One-Stop Planner**
Workshop 4: Research, cont. **Giving and Listening to an Informative Speech** **Give an Informative Speech** ❑ The Big Idea pp. 654–655 ❑ A Fine Organization pp. 655–657 ❑ Hitting the Perfect Note pp. 657–658 ❑ Stand and Deliver pp. 658–659 ❑ Practice & Apply 11 p. 659 **Listen to an Informative Speech** ❑ Before the Speech p. 659 ❑ During the Speech p. 659 ❑ After the Speech p. 660 ❑ Practice & Apply 12 p. 660	**Writing, Listening, & Speaking** ❑ Project-Planning Guide p. 98 ❑ LHD Think Sheet p. 99 ❑ LHD Sample Visuals Transparency 15 ❑ OLL Think Sheet p. 100 ❑ Evaluation Guide p. 101 ❑ Video Think Sheet pp. 102–103 **Lesson Plans for Language Development** ❑ p. 261	**Writing, Listening, & Speaking** ❑ Videocassette Segment 4 ❑ **One-Stop Planner**
Progress Assessment: Writing, Listening, & Speaking ❑ Analytical Scale and Scoring Rubric pp. 53–55		❑ **One-Stop Planner**
Workshop 4: Research, cont. ❑ Standards Practice and Review p. 661		
	Writing, Listening, & Speaking ❑ Choices p. 104 ❑ LHD Social Studies ❑ OLL Careers, Math ❑ AL Drama	❑ **One-Stop Planner**

HOLT LITERATURE & LANGUAGE ARTS

• **Red type** = Minimum Course of Study necessary to meet the California Standards
• **LHD** = Learners Having Difficulty (Benchmark/Strategic)   **OLL** = On-Level Learners   **AL** = Advanced Learners

Week 31, continued
Lesson Plan

Writing 1.6, 2.0
Listening and Speaking 1.0, 1.1, 1.2, 1.4, 1.5, 1.6, 1.7, 2.0, 2.3a, 2.3b, 2.3c, 2.3d
English-Language Conventions 1.0, 1.4, 1.5

GRADE 7: PUPIL'S EDITION AND HOLT HANDBOOK	STANDARDS–BASED COMPONENTS	SUPPORTING RESOURCES
Chapter 14: Punctuation, cont. ❑ Writing Application p. 317	**Language & Sentence Skills Practice** ❑ OLL, AL Proofreading Application p. 301 ❑ AL Literary Model pp. 302–303 ❑ AL Writing Application p. 304	❑ **One-Stop Planner**
Chapter 15: Punctuation ❑ Diagnostic Preview pp. 318–319 ❑ Underlining (Italics) pp. 320–322 ❑ Quotation Marks pp. 322–328	**Developmental Language & Sentence Skills** ❑ LHD pp. 115–120 **Language & Sentence Skills Practice** ❑ Choices p. 305 ❑ OLL pp. 306–313 **Lesson Plans for Language Development** ❑ p. 300	**At Home: A Guide to Standards Mastery** ❑ Using Quotation Marks p. 33 ❑ **One-Stop Planner**
	Spelling Lessons & Activities ❑ Unit 5 Review (Lesson 31) pp. 68–69	❑ **One-Stop Planner**

HOLT HANDBOOK

OPTIONAL   *Daily Language Activities Transparencies*

Transparency 18   Proofreading Warm-ups
Transparency 84   Sentence Combining

Teaching Notes

GRADE 7: PUPIL'S EDITION AND HOLT HANDBOOK	STANDARDS-BASED COMPONENTS	SUPPORTING RESOURCES
HOLT LITERATURE & LANGUAGE ARTS		
Mini-Workshop 2: Documenting Reference Sources pp. 697–699 ❑ Practice & Apply p. 699	**Writing, Listening, & Speaking** ❑ Document Reference Sources pp. 120–121 **Lesson Plans for Language Development** ❑ p. 267	❑ **One-Stop Planner**
Progress Assessment: Writing, Listening, & Speaking ❑ Analytical Scale p. 65		❑ **One-Stop Planner**
HOLT HANDBOOK **Chapter 15: Punctuation**, cont. ❑ Apostrophes pp. 330–337 ❑ Hyphens pp. 338–340 ❑ Parentheses pp. 340–341 ❑ Brackets p. 341 ❑ Dashes pp. 341–342 ❑ Chapter Review pp. 343–345 ❑ Writing Application p. 345	**Developmental Language & Sentence Skills** ❑ LHD pp. 121–124 **Language & Sentence Skills Practice** ❑ OLL pp. 314–325 ❑ OLL, AL Proofreading Application p. 326 ❑ AL Literary Model pp. 327–328 ❑ AL Writing Application p. 329 **Lesson Plans for Language Development** ❑ pp. 300–301	**At Home: A Guide to Standards Mastery** ❑ Using Hyphens p. 34 ❑ **One-Stop Planner**
ASSESSMENT **Progress Assessment: *Holt Handbook*** ❑ Chapter 15 Test pp. 29–30		**One-Stop Planner** ❑ Test Generator
	Spelling Lessons & Activities ❑ Lesson 32: More Greek Word Parts pp. 72–73	❑ **One-Stop Planner**

OPTIONAL *Daily Language Activities Transparencies*

Transparency 67   Analogies: Action : Acted Upon
Transparency 69   Analogies: Mixed

Review: To reinforce mastery of English-Language Convention Standard 1.4, have students complete Exercises 33–35 on pp. 403–404, Correcting Common Errors, in the *Holt Handbook.*

• **Red type** = Minimum Course of Study necessary to meet the California Standards
• **LHD** = Learners Having Difficulty (Benchmark/Strategic) **OLL** = On-Level Learners **AL** = Advanced Learners

Chapter 7 Overview
with Workshop 5, *Holt Handbook*

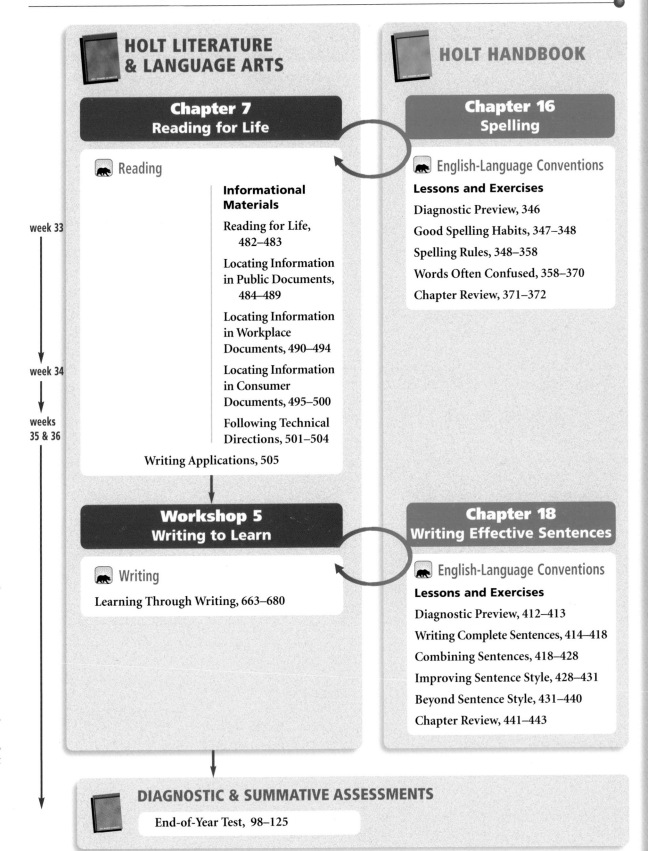

HOLT LITERATURE & LANGUAGE ARTS

Chapter 7
Reading for Life

Reading

week 33

week 34

weeks 35 & 36

Workshop 5
Writing to Learn

Writing

HOLT HANDBOOK

Chapter 16
Spelling

English-Language Conventions

Lessons and Exercises

Chapter 18
Writing Effective Sentences

English-Language Conventions

Lessons and Exercises

DIAGNOSTIC & SUMMATIVE ASSESSMENTS

GRADE 7: PUPIL'S EDITION AND HOLT HANDBOOK	STANDARDS-BASED COMPONENTS	SUPPORTING RESOURCES
Chapter 7: Reading for Life ❑ Reading for Life pp. 482–483	**Interactive Reading** ❑ Strategy Launch and Practice Read pp. 265–271 **Lesson Plans for Language Development** ❑ pp. 227–228	❑ **One-Stop Planner** ❑ **One-Stop Planner**

Informational Materials
❑ Locating Information in Public Documents pp. 484–489
  ❑ Casting Call p. 484
  ❑ Hollywood Beat p. 486
  ❑ Application for Permission to Work in the Entertainment Industry pp. 487–488
  ❑ Focus On: questions p. 489
	Interactive Reading
	❑ p. 272
	
	Lesson Plans for Language Development
	❑ pp. 229–232, 241
		❑ **One-Stop Planner**

Progress Assessment: Reading, Vocabulary, & Literature ❑ Locating Information in Public Documents pp. 173–174		**One-Stop Planner** ❑ Test Generator

Chapter 7: Reading for Life, cont.
 	
Informational Materials
❑ Locating Information in Workplace Documents pp. 490–494
  ❑ Letter from Casting Director p. 491
  ❑ Talent Instructions p. 492
  ❑ E-mail Memos and Directory p. 493
  ❑ Focus On: questions p. 494
	Interactive Reading
	❑ p. 273
	
	Lesson Plans for Language Development
	❑ pp. 233–235, 242, 245
		❑ **One-Stop Planner**

Progress Assessment: Reading, Vocabulary, & Literature ❑ Locating Information in Workplace Documents pp. 175–176		**One-Stop Planner** ❑ Test Generator

HOLT LITERATURE & LANGUAGE ARTS

- **Red type** = Minimum Course of Study necessary to meet the California Standards
- **LHD** = Learners Having Difficulty (Benchmark/Strategic) **OLL** = On-Level Learners **AL** = Advanced Learners

GRADE 7: PUPIL'S EDITION AND HOLT HANDBOOK	STANDARDS–BASED COMPONENTS	SUPPORTING RESOURCES
Chapter 16: Spelling ❑ Diagnostic Preview p. 346 ❑ Good Spelling Habits pp. 347–348 ❑ Spelling Rules pp. 348–350, 350–354, 354–355	**Developmental Language & Sentence Skills** ❑ LHD pp. 125–128 **Language & Sentence Skills Practice** ❑ Choices p. 330 ❑ OLL pp. 331–339 **Lesson Plans for Language Development** ❑ p. 302	**At Home: A Guide to Standards Mastery** ❑ Spelling with Prefixes p. 35 ❑ **One-Stop Planner**
	Spelling Lessons & Activities ❑ Lesson 33: Words with Many Syllables pp. 74–75	❑ **One-Stop Planner**

OPTIONAL *Daily Language Activities Transparencies*

Transparency 33   Vocabulary: Prefixes
Transparency 52   Analogies: Agent : Acted Upon
Transparency 78   Sentence Combining
Transparency 93   Critical Reading: Sentence Completions

Teaching Notes

GRADE 7: PUPIL'S EDITION AND HOLT HANDBOOK	STANDARDS–BASED COMPONENTS	SUPPORTING RESOURCES

Chapter 7: Reading for Life, cont.
 Informational Materials
 ❑ Locating Information in Consumer Documents pp. 495–500
   ❑ BART System Map p. 496
   ❑ BART's Bicycle Rules p. 497
   ❑ BART Ticket Guide p. 498
   ❑ BART Schedule p. 499
   ❑ Focus On: questions p. 500
	Interactive Reading
	 ❑ p. 274
	 Lesson Plans for Language Development
	 ❑ pp. 236–239, 243
		❑ **One-Stop Planner**

Progress Assessment: Reading, Vocabulary, & Literature ❑ Locating Information in Consumer Documents pp. 177–178		**One-Stop Planner** ❑ Test Generator
Chapter 16: Spelling, cont. ❑ Spelling Rules pp. 355–358 ❑ Words Often Confused pp. 358–370 ❑ Chapter Review pp. 371–372 ❑ Writing Application p. 373	**Developmental Language & Sentence Skills** ❑ LHD pp. 129–136 **Language & Sentence Skills Practice** ❑ OLL pp. 340–353 ❑ OLL, AL Proofreading Application p. 354 ❑ AL Literary Model pp. 355–356 ❑ AL Writing Application p. 357 **Lesson Plans for Language Development** ❑ pp. 302–303	❑ **One-Stop Planner**
ASSESSMENT **Progress Assessment:** *Holt Handbook* ❑ Chapter 16 Test pp. 31–32		**One-Stop Planner** ❑ Test Generator
	Spelling Lessons & Activities ❑ Lesson 34: More Latin Roots pp. 76–77	❑ **One-Stop Planner**

HOLT LITERATURE & LANGUAGE ARTS

HOLT HANDBOOK

OPTIONAL   *Daily Language Activities Transparencies*

Transparency 4	Proofreading Warm-ups
Transparency 29	Vocabulary: Frequently Confused Words
Transparency 53	Analogies: Action : Emotion
Transparency 101	Critical Reading: Passage Completions

Review: To reinforce mastery of English-Language Convention Standard 1.7, have students complete Exercises 36–37 on p. 405, Correcting Common Errors, in the *Holt Handbook*.

HOLT LITERATURE & LANGUAGE ARTS

GRADE 7: PUPIL'S EDITION AND HOLT HANDBOOK	STANDARDS-BASED COMPONENTS	SUPPORTING RESOURCES

Chapter 7: Reading for Life, cont.
Informational Material
❑ Following Technical Directions pp. 501–504
  ❑ How to Change a Flat Tire pp. 502–503
  ❑ Focus On: questions p. 504
	Interactive Reading
	❑ p. 275
	Lesson Plans for Language Development
	❑ pp. 240, 244, 246
		❑ **One-Stop Planner**

Progress Assessment: Reading, Vocabulary, & Literature ❑ Following Technical Directions pp. 179–180		**One-Stop Planner** ❑ Test Generator
	Interactive Reading ❑ OLL Make Your Money Grow pp. 276–283 ❑ OLL A Sample Business Plan pp. 284–288 ❑ OLL How to Locate the Big and Little Dippers pp. 289–294 ❑ OLL California State Parks: Rules and Regulations pp. 295–299	❑ **One-Stop Planner**

ASSESSMENT
Progress Assessment: Reading, Vocabulary, & Literature
❑ Chapter Test
  ❑ Part A: Informational Response and Analysis pp. 181–182
  ❑ Part B: Reading Application pp. 183–187
		One-Stop Planner
		❑ Test Generator

Chapter 7: Reading for Life, cont. ❑ Writing Applications: Summary p. 505		

• **Red type** = Minimum Course of Study necessary to meet the California Standards
• **LHD** = Learners Having Difficulty (Benchmark/Strategic)   **OLL** = On-Level Learners   **AL** = Advanced Learners

GRADE 7: PUPIL'S EDITION AND HOLT HANDBOOK	STANDARDS-BASED COMPONENTS	SUPPORTING RESOURCES
HOLT LIT & LANGUAGE ARTS **Workshop 5: Writing to Learn** **Learning Through Writing** pp. 663–680 Summaries pp. 663–669 ❑ Practice & Apply 1 p. 669 Databases pp. 669–672 ❑ Practice & Apply 2 p. 672 Spreadsheets pp. 672–675 ❑ Practice & Apply 3 p. 675	**Writing, Listening, & Speaking** ❑ LHD, OLL Write a Summary p. 106 ❑ OLL Create a Database p. 107 ❑ OLL, AL Create a Spreadsheet pp. 108–109 **Lesson Plans for Language Development** ❑ pp. 262–263	❑ **One-Stop Planner**
Progress Assessment: Writing, Listening, & Speaking ❑ Analytical Scale and Rubrics pp. 56–61		❑ **One-Stop Planner**
HOLT HANDBOOK **Chapter 18: Writing Effective Sentences** ❑ Diagnostic Preview pp. 412–413 ❑ Writing Complete Sentences pp. 414–418 ❑ Combining Sentences pp. 418–428	**Developmental Language & Sentence Skills** ❑ LHD pp. 139–148 **Language & Sentence Skills Practice** ❑ OLL pp. 399–420 **Lesson Plans for Language Development** ❑ pp. 306–307	**At Home: A Guide to Standards Mastery** ❑ Using Infinitives in Sentences p. 36 ❑ **One-Stop Planner**
	Spelling Lessons & Activities ❑ Lesson 35: Noun Suffixes pp. 78–79	❑ **One-Stop Planner**

OPTIONAL *Daily Language Activities Transparencies*

Transparency 19	Proofreading Warm-ups
Transparency 39	Vocabulary: Synonyms
Transparency 56	Analogies: Action : Acted Upon
Transparency 109	Critical Reading: Passage Analysis

Teaching Notes

GRADE 7: PUPIL'S EDITION AND HOLT HANDBOOK	STANDARDS-BASED COMPONENTS	SUPPORTING RESOURCES
Workshop 5: Writing to Learn, cont. **Learning Through Writing** Word-Processing and Publishing Features pp. 675–680 ❑ Practice & Apply 4 p. 680	**Writing, Listening, & Speaking** ❑ OLL Use Word-Processing or Publishing Software p. 110 **Lesson Plans for Language Development** ❑ pp. 262–263	❑ **One-Stop Planner**
ASSESSMENT **Progress Assessment: Writing, Listening, & Speaking** ❑ Writing Workshop 5 Test pp. 14–18 ❑ Analytical Scale and Rubric pp. 62–63		❑ **One-Stop Planner**

	Writing, Listening, & Speaking
	❑ Choices p. 111
	  ❑ LHD Summaries
	  ❑ OLL Databases, Publishing Features
	  ❑ AL Spreadsheets
		❑ **One-Stop Planner**

Workshop 5: Writing to Learn, cont. ❑ Standards Practice and Review p. 681		
Chapter 18: Writing Effective Sentences, cont. ❑ Improving Sentence Style pp. 428–431 ❑ Beyond Sentence Style pp. 431–439, 439–440 ❑ Chapter Review pp. 441–443	**Developmental Language & Sentence Skills** ❑ LHD pp. 149–156 **Language & Sentence Skills Practice** ❑ OLL pp. 421–430 **Lesson Plans for Language Development** ❑ p. 307	❑ **One-Stop Planner**
ASSESSMENT **Progress Assessment: *Holt Handbook*** ❑ Chapter 18 Test pp. 35–38		**One-Stop Planner** ❑ Test Generator

HOLT LITERATURE & LANGUAGE ARTS

HOLT HANDBOOK

• **Red type** = Minimum Course of Study necessary to meet the California Standards
• **LHD** = Learners Having Difficulty (Benchmark/Strategic) **OLL** = On-Level Learners **AL** = Advanced Learners

87

GRADE 7: PUPIL'S EDITION AND HOLT HANDBOOK	STANDARDS–BASED COMPONENTS	SUPPORTING RESOURCES
	Spelling Lessons & Activities ❏ Unit 6 Review (Lesson 36) pp. 80–81	❏ **One-Stop Planner**
		At Home: A Guide to Standards Mastery ❏ Keeping the Summer Productive: Encouraging Independent Reading p. 12 ❏ **One-Stop Planner**
ASSESSMENT **Diagnostic & Summative Assessments** ❏ End-of-Year Test pp. 98–125		**One-Stop Planner** ❏ Test Generator

OPTIONAL *Daily Language Activities Transparencies*

Transparency 20	Proofreading Warm-ups
Transparency 42	Vocabulary: Definitions
Transparency 70	Analogies: Variety
Transparency 85	Sentence Combining

Review: To reinforce mastery of English-Language Convention Standard 1.3, have students complete Exercises 1–7 on pp. 377–382, Correcting Common Errors, in the *Holt Handbook.*

- **Red type** = Minimum Course of Study necessary to meet the California Standards
- **LHD** = Learners Having Difficulty (Benchmark/Strategic)   **OLL** = On-Level Learners   **AL** = Advanced Learners